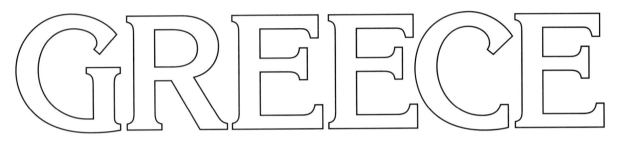

GREECE

· DISCOVERING THE PAST ·

by Jim Parsons, John Ewing, and Alex Newhart

REIDMORE BOOKS

About the Authors...

John Ewing is working on a master's degree in social studies and curriculum design at the University of Alberta. He is also currently teaching language arts to junior high students in Edmonton. In the future, he plans to complete a doctorate.

Alex Newhart has been an elementary school teacher for the County of Strathcona for 20 years. He currently is teaching grade 6 students at Pine Street School in Sherwood Park, Alberta.

Jim Parsons has been a professor for 15 years at the University of Alberta in the Department of Secondary Education. His specialties include social studies, literature, research, and religious education. When he was a teacher, he taught junior high social studies and language arts. Jim Parsons has written over 20 books, numerous educational articles, and has presented a number of workshops throughout North America.

Reidmore Books wishes to thank the following people for their insights and support in the development of this textbook:

Pedagogical Consultant

Marilyn Shortt
Greece: Discovering the Past
Project Social Studies Consultant
Roman Catholic Separate School District No. 7
Edmonton, Alberta

Academic Consultants

Dr. Donald Baronowski
Assistant Professor, Department of Classics
McGill University

Shari Lee Saunders, MA
Athabasca University

Dr. James Schovanek
Professor, Department of Classics
University of Alberta

Canadian Cataloguing in Publication Data

Parsons, Jim, 1948-
    Greece: discovering the past

    Includes index.
    ISBN 1-895073-17-0

    1. Greece—History—To 146 B.C.—Juvenile literature.
2. Greece—Civilization—To 146 B.C.—Juvenile literature.
I. Newhart, Alex, 1949- II. Ewing, John, 1957- III. Title.
DF215.P37 1992   938   C92-091278-8

Reidmore Books, Inc.
1200 Energy Square
10109 - 106 Street
Edmonton, Alberta T5J 3L7

printed in Canada

Contents

Preface

A LETTER TO THE STUDENTS FROM THE AUTHORS

HAVE you ever wondered who came up with the idea of playing hockey? Why do people in Canada drive on the right side of the road and people in some other countries drive on the left? Why do young people have "their" music and older people have "theirs?" Why is Canada's government the way it is? Who were the first doctors? There are many mysteries and unanswered questions in our world. How do you solve these mysteries? How do you find the answers to these questions?

You will learn in this book that there are many different ways to find the answers to questions. The questions may be the same, but the answers may differ. One reason answers differ is that many people have become **specialists**. They answer questions from a specific, or special, point of view.

Have you wondered why you study social studies during one part of your school day and science during another part? The answer is that social studies is one subject, and science is another. People who work in these separate subject areas are interested in different things. They may study the same civilization—such as ancient Greece—but they will probably study different parts of it.

Social studies helps us answer questions like those listed in the first paragraph. Answering questions does more than just satisfy our curiosity. If we could not answer questions about why things are like they are, it would be hard to make good decisions about even the most simple things. It may seem odd, but studying ancient Greece will help you to answer questions about your life right now.

Because people in two subject areas study different parts of the same civilization, they try to answer different questions. A **sociologist** will ask why people live in groups. A **psychologist** will ask how people learn to think. You might call these different people detectives. These detectives use different clues to help them answer the questions they care about.

For example, archaeologists look at the ruins of old civilizations. These ruins may lay hidden under hundreds or even thousands of years of dirt and soil. By looking at the clues they find, archaeologists try to put together a picture of what life must have been like in those earlier days.

Historians and archaeologists are also like detectives. They have one thing in common. They want to know if the mysteries they solve will help them learn something new and important. Did you know that for a long time no one believed the ancient city of Troy was a real city? Many people thought Troy was only a legend. But archaeologists found the city and a new door was unlocked.

As you read this book, you will be the archaeologist looking for clues. To learn about ancient Greece, where should you begin? One way to begin might be to write down everything you already know about the subject you are studying—ancient Greece. See how many pieces of the puzzle you already know.

A second step might be to think of areas you know very little about. But how do you know what you don't know if you don't know it? One way to look at the ancient world is to think about your world.

For example, what clothes do you wear? What do you eat? Where is your country on the map? These are good questions to start with. Write the answers to these questions into a notebook you can call your **archaeologist's journal**. You will probably need to dig for more evidence. Where can you look?

This textbook is built to help you on your archaeological dig. At the beginning of every chapter, you will find some questions that ask you to "dig up" some information about ancient Greece. The chief archaeologist (your teacher) will also give you specific areas to look at. Do you wonder if some child in ancient Greece had to do this? The answer is yes. Young people in ancient Greece had to learn

things, too. Their schools were different from yours, but they studied as hard. How different were their schools? In this book, you will find out.

Why do you study ancient Greece? One reason is that a study of ancient Greece is a great way to sharpen your skills as a detective. As you sharpen your skills, you will be ready to learn other things. Perhaps, someday, you will discover the sunken city of Atlantis. Purely fiction? Don't forget the discovery of Troy!

A LETTER TO THE TEACHERS FROM THE AUTHORS

Using the Book

Before you begin to use this book, we'd like to tell you how we put it together so that you might understand how to use it better. All three of us are teachers, and we've tried to make the layout of the book as helpful to you as possible. We have put together the elements of the book in ways we think are "teachable." We tried to create a book we would like to use ourselves.

As you read the book, you will find the same structure in each chapter. That is, each chapter has elements such as Digging Up questions, Key Concepts, Key Facts, maps, summaries, boldface vocabulary highlights for unusual or difficult words, pictures, and questions. There are also sidebars and case studies.

Using the Visuals

We believe that the artist who drew the pictures for us did beautiful work. But we also believe that pictures should be more than just decorative. We think students can use them to learn. So, when you look at the pictures and maps, you will see that each caption has three elements. The first sentence of the caption states a fact about ancient Greece. The second sentence is a question asking students to analyze the picture more thoroughly and think about what they see. The third sentence is a project question asking students to go beyond the picture to discover additional information. Of course, you need not use all our questions. But we wrote them because we believed they would be helpful to us as we taught the book.

Inquiry

As you read this book, you will find that it is written in a particular way. First, we believe that knowing things is important, and we have tried to fill the book with information. Second, we have tried to write the book so students will enjoy reading it. For example, we liked many myths and legends of the ancient Greeks. So we have written the ones in this book in story form instead of typical textbook narration.

Third, and most important of all, we have put the textbook together in a way that stresses inquiry. For us, inquiry is more than a method. It is a belief system about teaching that manifests itself in the way teaching is organized. We also believe that the more students know, the more intellectually mature they become. We believe that intellectual maturity is the goal of education.

We believe that good students are naturally curious. We teachers understand the value of sharing goals and objectives with students. We believe students should have an opportunity to know what this book is about, how it is put together, and why it is organized as it is. We also believe that students can understand what is happening in their classes. For this reason, we have written a letter specifically to them and we have placed this letter to teachers where students can read it.

This textbook is an inquiry textbook. That is, we have tried to organize the entire structure of the text around a belief in inquiry. Special features in the book aid the inquiry approach. All chapters open with **Digging Up** questions that invite students to think like archaeologists. These questions ask the students about their own lives and to "dig up" information about ancient Greece as they read the chapter. As well, most **headings** within chapters pose questions that help organize students' thinking and exploration as they read. **Visuals** ask them to explore further. **Wrapping Up** questions at the end of each chapter are organized around specific inquiry strategies. **Developing Your Skills** sections offer activities that help build students' learning skills. Also at the end of each chapter is a **Moving On** section that helps students pull together what they have learned. The **Moving On** section also helps students organize their study of the next chapter.

To help you understand the terms we use in this text, we have provided the following definitions.

GENERALIZATION: A principle that shows relationships between two or more concepts.

CONCEPT: An idea or meaning, represented by a word, term, or other symbol, which stands for a class or group of things.

FACT: A part or piece of information that applies to specific situations. For example, facts include specific statements about people, things, events, or ideas.

KEY CONCEPT: A principle that is universally true in all civilizations. A key concept provides a link between the civilization of ancient Greece and our present-day civilization. A key concept seeks to have students ask the question, "If this is true of yesterday, could it also be true today?"

KEY FACT: A statement of fact that relates directly to the text. A key fact provides specific and concise information about the content your students will be studying. Key facts are the "Did you know" of the text. They seek to present cause-and-effect relationships in ancient Greece.

We hope that the structure of our text is both simple and complete. Throughout the book, we have created opportunities for students to use their imagination and inquiry skills.

Question Strategies

Each **Wrapping Up** section in the book has a six-question format, organized in the following hierarchy of questioning.

Question One asks students to remember what they have learned.

Question Two asks students to evaluate how well they have understood the text.

Question Three asks students to apply what they have learned.

Question Four asks students to analyze new information, or old information in a new way.

Question Five asks students to pull together what they have learned and construct new ideas.

Question Six asks students to think for themselves and evaluate what they have studied.

The questions included in each section of the book were created to help students develop a hierarchy of skills. They were also intended to draw answers that direct students towards important social studies concepts (for example, what do the questions tell us about civilization?). Our attempt has been to bring what the students learn from studying ancient Greece into a modern setting, which helps address their most current social studies curriculum needs.

We hope that you enjoy using this textbook. But, most of all, we hope that our work helps your students learn more about ancient Greece and, as they do, become more intellectually mature and able learners as they do so.

Jim Parsons
Alex Newhart
John Ewing

PART

II

Introduction

The first part of this book will introduce you to the study of ancient Greece. You will learn about some contributions that ancient Greeks have made to Western civilization. Then you will read an overview of early Greek history, and learn how historians and archaeologists have discovered the history of Greece. Then you will read about something that is almost the same today as in ancient times: the geography and climate of Greece.

An Introduction to Ancient Greece

DIGGING UP

1. Have you ever studied your family's past? What do you know about your grand-parents and their lives when they were your age?
2. Why is knowing something about the past important?
3. Ancient Greece has influenced Western civilizations in many ways. As you read this chapter, "dig up" several ways ancient Greece has affected our lives.

WHY ARE WE STUDYING ANCIENT GREECE?

THIS book is about ancient Greece. The word **ancient** means old. The **civilization** of ancient Greece was one of the world's earliest civilizations. It was such an important civilization that most young people study it in their school life. But that special civilization is now dead and gone.

That we are studying this ancient civilization at all probably brings an important question to your mind. Why would you want to study the history of a civilization that is dead and gone? There are many reasons to study the history of ancient Greece. One important reason is that our civilization owes a great deal to the ancient Greeks. Like a footprint left in sand, or a fossil, the ancient Greeks have left their footprints in our **heritage**.

We are not exactly like the ancient Greeks, just as you are not exactly like your grandfather or grandmother. Still, you share many things with your grandparents. In the same way, our modern civilization shares many characteristics with ancient Greece. Some shared characteristics are the political ideas of **democracy**, and the philosophical and educational ideas of important Greek thinkers such as Aristotle and Socrates. Other shared characteristics are the myths and stories of gods and goddesses, a belief in the importance of a strong mind and body, and the Olympics.

 KEY CONCEPTS
> By studying ancient Greece, we can learn more about our own lives.

KEY FACTS
> The ancient Greek civilization can help us to understand how **Western** civilizations started, grew, and prospered. The ancient Greek civilization has influenced our art, architecture, and language.

Greece in the World Today

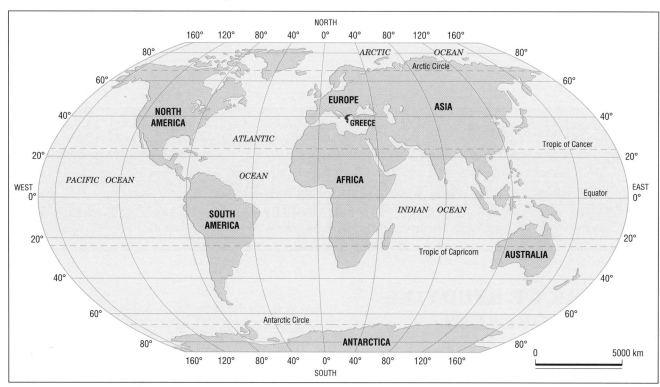

- *Modern Greece is a country in southeastern Europe.*
- *What is the latitude and longitude of modern Greece?*
- *What is the distance between modern Greece and your country?*

In this book, you will discover many things about ancient Greece that will remind you of our civilization. You will also study many ways that our civilization differs from ancient Greece. As you read, your teacher may want you to keep a list of **similarities** and **differences** in your notebook. But even if you don't keep a special list, you can consider these points yourself. Why? Because knowing more about the people of ancient Greece helps you know more about yourself.

What's the Difference Between BC and AD?

As you read this book, you will notice that the years seem to go backwards. The 5th century BC (starting in 500 BC) is older than the 4th century BC (starting in 400 BC). Don't be confused. Sorting out the years is easy.

The history of the world is often separated into two sections: BC (Before Christ) and AD (Anno Domini — meaning "in the year of our Lord" in Latin). The history of ancient Greece takes place before the birth of Jesus (in the year 1). Years before Jesus was born are counted backwards from the year 1. Years since the birth of Jesus are counted forwards from the year 1. Thus, the year before Jesus' birth was the year 1 BC.

In the year 500 BC, ancient Greece was a powerful civilization, meaning that ancient Greece was powerful 500 years before Jesus was born. The great Greek poet Homer was born about 800 BC, meaning that Homer was about 800 years older than Jesus.

What Do We Owe the Ancient Greeks?

Ancient Greece has affected our lives more than any other ancient civilization. Here's a Top 10 Chart called "Things the Ancient Greeks Have Given to Us." As you read the book, see what else you might add to our list. Make your own Top 25 Chart. You might even want to replace some of our points with ones of your own.

1. The ancient Greeks have given us one of our most prized ideals: democracy.

2. The ancient Greeks have given us the basis for our science and medicine. (Modern medicine owes much to Hippocrates' belief in investigation and observation.)

3. The ancient Greeks have given us the modern play.

4. The ancient Greek **philosophers** such as Socrates, Plato, and Aristotle have given us many of our philosophical beliefs.

5. The ancient Greeks influenced our art and sculpture.

6. The ancient Greeks have given us the Olympic games.

7. The ancient Greeks have given us myths of **heroes**, gods, and goddesses, which have been handed down through centuries and are told almost every day to young people around the world.

8. The ancient Greeks have given us our belief in a healthy body.

9. The ancient Greeks' love of learning has given us our educational system.

10. The ancient Greek civilization influenced other civilizations, such as the Roman, which also influenced us.

Ancient Greek Influences on Modern Life

- *Our society owes much of its culture to the ancient Greeks.*
- *Each of these four pictures highlights part of our society that is influenced by ancient Greece. Can you name the influences?*
- *List five things you like to do. Pick one of these. Then look up the history of the activity (or thing) you have chosen. Where does it come from? Is it based on the activities of some other group?*

WRAPPING UP

1. Throughout this book, we call Greece an *ancient* civilization. Why do we call it *ancient*?

2. In your own words, write a paragraph explaining the difference between BC and AD.

3. (a) As a group, look up one of the following civilizations in an encyclopedia: the Romans, the Persians, the Babylonians, or the Chinese (dynasties).

(b) Quickly read the section on the group you have chosen.

(c) As you read, list five to ten dates and events that are listed as important to this civilization. (Make sure some are AD and some are BC).

(d) With the dates you have written down, make a time line of the important events and their dates. (Later, you might compare your time line with one of ancient Greece to see similarities and differences.)

4. (a) Write down the words civilization, heritage, and democracy.

(b) Without looking them up, write your own definitions of these words.

(c) Now, look up these three words in the glossary. Compare your own definitions with the definitions you find. How different are they?

(d) Using what you have learned, rewrite your definitions (if they need to be rewritten).

(e) Copy these definitions into your notebook (your archaeologist's journal).

5. In your notebook, start a Top 25 Chart called "Things the Ancient Greeks Have Given Us." As you read each chapter in your text, add one or two things to your chart. Make sure that you keep your chart up to date. Get into the habit of taking these notes.

6. (a) Reread the Top 10 Chart called "Things the Ancient Greeks Have Given to Us."

(b) Using your own ideas about what is important, put the list in order of importance, starting with the most important. Write down why you made your choices.

(c) Write down what you think are the Top Five contributions of the ancient Greeks.

(d) Compare your list with the lists of your classmates. How are they similar or different?

DEVELOPING YOUR SKILLS

1. (a) Conduct a brief, one-question survey with three adults you know. The one question you will ask is: "What Do We Owe the Ancient Greeks?"

(b) After you have asked the question, collect your answers. As a class, compile the answers to see what most people said.

(c) As a class, answer the questions: What did you find out from your survey? Why do you think people answered the question the way they did? Explain.

MOVING ON

In this chapter, you learned many things about ancient Greece. For example, you learned that our modern civilization shares many characteristics with that of ancient Greece. We have already told you that one of the goals of your study is to learn more about ancient Greece so you can learn more about your society. For this reason, we suggested that you keep a list of similarities and differences in your notebook.

To learn more about ancient Greece, where could you go from here? One choice is to start with the history of ancient Greece. Before we can understand why people did the things they did, we must understand the time, or the **context**, in which they lived. We must also understand the people, places, and events that influenced their lives. The next chapter gives an overview of ancient Greek history to help us make a path to follow during the rest of our study.

CHAPTER 2

An Overview of Ancient Greek History

DIGGING UP

1. Countries, like people, are always changing. Is your country going through changes? If so, what are the changes?
2. In the history of ancient Greece, many civilizations grew and changed. Which period of ancient Greek civilization do we know the most about? As you read this chapter, "dig up" some reasons this period was important.

WHEN DID CIVILIZATION IN ANCIENT GREECE BEGIN?

MANY early civilizations have lived at different times in the area we call Greece. In this chapter, you will learn about several civilizations that led to the development of ancient Greek civilization. While you read, make a time line of history in ancient Greece.

The history of civilization in ancient Greece begins about 3000 BC. Around that time, three groups of peoples—known today as the Aegean civilization—lived near what is now modern Greece. One civilization developed on the island of Crete. These people were the **Minoans**.

The second group of people lived on the **mainland**. They were **Helladic**. The third group of people lived in the Aegean island area. They were **Cycladic**. Although this book will focus mainly on the Minoan and Helladic cultures, remember that each group of people had an influence on forming ancient Greek civilization.

THE BRONZE AGE

Can you picture an early **Bronze Age** civilization in your mind? Early people lived quite differently from the way we live today. For example, they did not have the modern **conveniences** many of us have.

Why Is the Bronze Age Called the Bronze Age?

Bronze is a metal. The best bronze is a mixture of copper and a little tin. Other **alloys** can be added to copper to make bronze. These include lead, antimony, and arsenic. Today, bronze is used mostly in art and sculpting.

The Bronze Age is a period of very early history. It lasted from about 3000 to 1050 BC. During the Bronze Age, humans learned to make bronze tools, to use the wheel, and to plough the land with oxen. Because people in the Bronze Age learned how to use a metal such as bronze instead of stone, they could build stronger tools. Bronze tools helped them grow more crops and trade with other **cultures**. As a result, civilizations grew and expanded.

Bronze tools had two major advantages over stone tools. First, bronze was easier than stone to shape into tools. Second, bronze was not as brittle as stone.

KEY CONCEPTS

The development of a society is a slow and difficult process. One way to study an early civilization is to look at how it grew.

Even in Bronze Age Greece, the people were starting to develop a great civilization. One of the earliest known civilizations lasted more than 1500 years before it gradually declined, and another civilization came to dominate over the area. This early civilization was the Minoan civilization.

The Minoan Civilization

Crete is the largest island in Greece. It is an island of mountains. Today, sheep and goats roam through the hilly countryside. Crete is a popular vacation spot for many people.

Crete wasn't always like it is today. A long time ago, Crete was the home of one of the most advanced civilizations in the world. Crete's history started at the beginning of the Bronze Age.

The Minoan civilization on Crete grew and prospered because it discovered two important **technologies**. One important technology was how to use metal, and the other was how to write.

First, the Minoans discovered how to dig metal from the ground and turn it into tools. Metal tools are stronger than stone tools.

Second, the Minoans developed a way of writing using pictures. The script they developed is called **pictography**. It was often simple, but it was useful. Using pictures, the Minoans could write and keep records.

Together, these two important technologies allowed the Minoans to build great buildings and boats and to trade with other people by sea.

• *Ancient people who learned to write left behind valuable records for us to study.*
• *How do you think this script was marked onto the stone?*
• *What kinds of things can people today learn from ancient writings?*

As early as 2200 BC, the cities of Crete were large and busy. Minoan art and architecture developed into beautiful art forms.

Archaeologists believe that about 1450 BC a **natural disaster** destroyed the main cities of Crete. After the destruction of its cities, Crete never again had a powerful civilization. Instead, people on the mainland of Greece grew powerful.

The Mycenaean Civilization

Around 1600 BC to 1200 BC, one city on the mainland of Greece was the most powerful. The city was Mycenae. The Mycenaean civilization was important during the late Bronze Age.

Like many civilizations, the Mycenaeans adopted the best ideas of other people. They copied much of their architecture from the Minoans on Crete. The Mycenaeans also developed many of their own types of structures.

 **KEY FACTS**

When a civilization dies, it is not completely dead. The civilizations that follow use what they have learned from this early civilization to develop their own. For example, the civilization of Mycenae used many things they had learned from the Minoans.

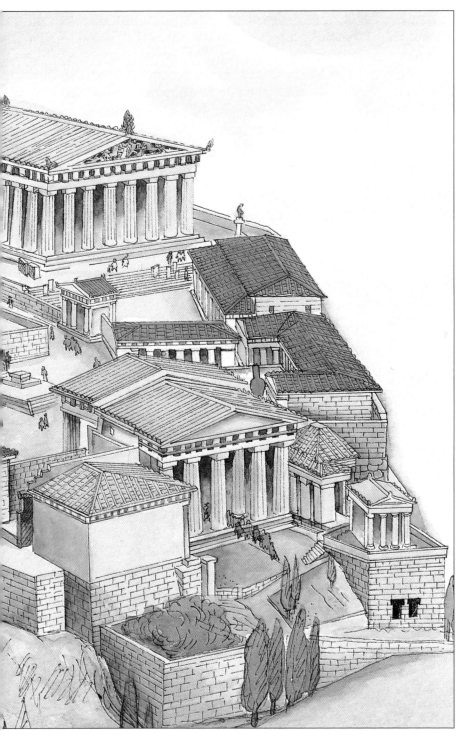

- *The Acropolis in Athens was a hill in the middle of the* **city-state**.
- *Using this picture, estimate the height and length of the buildings. How did you figure out your answer?*
- *Why were the buildings in this picture built on a high hill?*

They were great city planners. One of their best ideas was to build a city around a high hill, which could be fortified. The high hill was called the **acropolis**. Later Greek city-states continued this plan for cities.

Mycenae was the home of **King Agamemnon**. It was also where many Greek legends came from. For example, the legends of the **Trojan Horse** and Helen of Troy came from Mycenae.

Eventually, Mycenae was invaded by the **Dorians**. Historians say that the civilization of Mycenae had ended by 1100 BC.

THE DARK AGES AND ARCHAIC PERIOD

 KEY FACTS — The **Dark Ages** lasted from about 1050 to 900 BC.

After the civilizations of Mycenae and Crete were destroyed, ancient Greece "moved" into the Dark Ages. This period of time is called the Dark Ages because we know very little about what happened during it. We are "in the dark." What we do know is that most building and trade stopped. The people became poor and struggled to survive.

During the Dark Ages, the people of the Mediterranean world constantly fought with each other. The early Greeks belonged to different groups. Each group spoke a different **dialect**. Throughout Greece,

Babylonia, coastal Asia Minor, and Egypt there were many wars. Some groups became strong and powerful. Others became weak. These wars also caused many people to move and settle in different areas.

The Dorians and Ionians

About 1100 BC, the Dorians, a group of northern Greeks, began to invade the rest of Greece. The Dorians left their mountain homes and moved down through the mainland of Greece. Some Dorians moved to the island of Crete.

The Dorians had one thing that made them stronger than the people they met: they had iron weapons. Iron weapons are stronger than even bronze weapons.

Using these iron weapons, the Dorians managed to conquer many of the Mycenaean settlements. Other Mycenaeans united with the

Important Sites in the Ancient Greek World

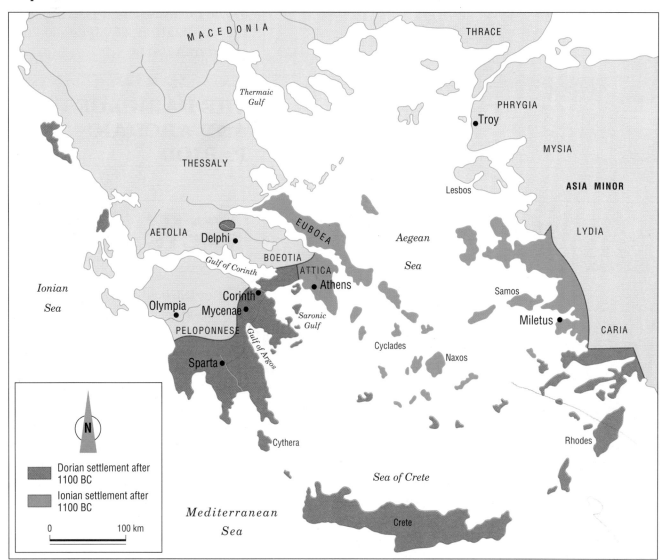

• *This map shows sites which were important at different times of Greek history. You can refer to it often during your study of ancient Greece.*

• *Using the scale, measure how far someone would have to travel to get from Athens to Olympia.*

• *Using the legend, find where the Dorians and **Ionians** lived after 1100 BC. Explain why they lived there.*

Dorians. Finally, the Dorians settled in the southern and eastern parts of the Greek **peninsula**. Sparta and Corinth became the most important Dorian cities of mainland Greece. The Dorians also founded other Greek city-states. They were a strong people and helped the Greeks become a military power.

The Ionians lived in the middle of Greece. When the Dorians conquered Greece from the north, most of the Ionians fled to the islands and to the coast of Asia Minor. Here, they developed important Greek cities and developed their own culture.

Ionian history is very important because of the many contributions the Ionians made to the Greek civilization. Ionians contributed the Ionic style of Greek architecture and many beautiful sculptures. They produced many great philosophers. The great poet Homer was an Ionian.

At the end of the Dark Ages, civilization in Greece entered a time known as the Archaic Period. The Archaic Period lasted from about 900 to 550 BC. At this time, a civilization which came to be called the ancient Greek civilization grew. The only written histories we have of these times are poems. One of ancient Greece's greatest poets was Homer. Homer lived in Ionia about 750-700 BC. Some historians say that Homer's writing marks the light at the end of the Dark Ages. Today, over two thousand years later, people still marvel at the beauty of Homer's poetry.

THE CLASSICAL PERIOD

The history of ancient Greece is a long one. Most of what we know about ancient Greece comes from only one period. This period was called the **Classical Period**. It lasted from about 550 to 300 BC. Ancient Greece became one of the most important powers in the ancient world at this time.

During the Classical Period, the Greek peninsula was organized into many city-states. Two of these city-states were much stronger than the others. These two large, important city-states were Athens and Sparta.

The Classical Period was when the ancient Greeks built their strongest governments, social structures, buildings, and expanded their trade. You will learn more about these things later in this book.

After the Classical Period, ancient Greece made great military advances under the leadership of Alexander the Great. The life of Alexander the Great marks the beginning of the **Hellenistic Period**.

THE HELLENISTIC PERIOD

The civilization of ancient Greece was powerful, but it was like the civilizations before it in that it did not last forever. After the Classical Period, Greek power declined. In its place, Rome grew more powerful and finally conquered the ancient Greeks. Like so many civilizations before it, ancient Greece was absorbed into another civilization.

Why did the ancient Greek civilization die? The city-states fought with each other, which made them weak. Through a series of conquests, the Roman armies gradually conquered the ancient Greek civilization. From 334 BC to 264 BC, Rome controlled the Italian peninsula south of the Po River. Around 146 BC, Rome took over Macedonia and Greece. Greece became a Roman province.

Eventually, the Romans conquered much of Alexander the Great's old empire, including all of ancient Greece. (You will read more about Alexander the Great and his empire in chapter 18.) The date 30 BC marks the end of the Hellenistic Period.

WHAT WAS THE INFLUENCE OF ANCIENT GREECE?

Remember that when a civilization dies it is not completely dead. The ancient Greek city-states are gone, but the Greek civilization has lasted for centuries. Many parts of the ancient Greek civilization still exist.

Rome became the world's next great civilization. Because the Romans appreciated the Greek culture, they adopted some of it as their own. For example, the Romans loved Greek architecture, poetry, law, and philosophy. Even the Roman gods were patterned after the Greek gods. The Romans conquered the Greeks, but they encouraged and extended the Greek culture.

Many Greeks became Roman subjects. Many Greek teachers and advisors offered their services to Rome. In this way, the Greeks influenced the Roman culture. The ancient Greek culture and way of thinking survived because it was passed on to the Romans.

WRAPPING UP

1. Why did the Minoan civilization grow and prosper?
2. Reread the section called "Why Is the Bronze Age Called the Bronze Age?" In your own words, rewrite the section in three sentences. Make sure you get the most important points.
3. (a) Create a small chart with the title "What the Romans Owe the Greeks."
   (b) From the chapter, list as many things as you can find to fill in the chart.

4. This chapter gives information about the following civilizations: the Minoans, the Dorians, the Ionians, the Greeks, the Mycenaeans, and the Romans.
   (a) Put these civilizations in order, from the earliest to the latest.
   (b) Beside each group, write an interesting fact about it.
5. Do you think our civilization will last forever? What parts of it do you think a new civilization would adopt?
6. Read the following paragraph, then answer this question: From what you have read in this chapter, do you believe the ideas in the paragraph are true or false? Write true or false, then give reasons for your answer.

In the past 20 years, today's world has suddenly become modern. The world became modern all at once, instead of in a slow, step-by-step way. In the same way, "modern" Roman civilization quickly replaced the "old-fashioned" civilization of the Greeks.

DEVELOPING YOUR SKILLS

1. Look at a physical map of Greece. How does the landscape of Greece suggest why the Greeks organized themselves into city-states? Choose another country in the world with a different physical landscape. Find out what type of organization its people had. What does this tell you about physical landscape and how peoples organize themselves?

MOVING ON

In this chapter, you learned that ancient Greece grew like many other civilizations. This growth was gradual and slow. As ancient Greece grew and changed, it borrowed from other civilization. The result was that a new civilization emerged, one that was very different from the original one.

You learned that the influences of the Minoans, Mycenaeans, Dorians, and Ionians all worked together to establish a new and strong civilization. You also learned that no civilization dies completely. Ideas and ways of doing things are often passed on to later civilizations.

Before we take a closer look at ancient Greece, you must learn about and use the right instruments for the search. In the next chapter, we will tell you about two ways of finding out about past civilizations. You will learn how **historians** and **archaeologists** have helped us learn about the ancient Greeks.

Studying Ancient Greece

DIGGING UP

1. Have you ever read a book or seen a movie about a historian or an archaeologist?
2. What do you know about what historians and archaeologists do?
3. As you read this chapter, "dig up" at least one thing that most historians and archaeologists have in common.

WHAT DO HISTORIANS DO?

HISTORIANS are people who study the past. They help us organize the past so we can make sense of what we remember. When historians work, they follow a specific procedure that helps them find things out.

Historians have three jobs. Their first job is to record the events of the past. Their second job is to pass their records from one generation to another. But history is more than just memories. If these memories of the past are not organized, they would not make sense. So, the third job of the historian is to organize the past and help us make sense of what has happened.

KEY CONCEPTS

We can learn about ancient civilizations by studying the work of historians and archaeologists. Historians and archaeologists help us to understand ancient civilizations. They study ancient artifacts, such as pottery, jewellery, coins, buildings, art, poetry, historical records, and other remains of the earlier society. Each thing a society makes tells us something about that society.

Human beings want to remember the past for some important reasons. First, having a past lets us know who we are and where we came from. For example, much of what you are begins with the experiences of your parents and family.

Second, humans want to learn from the past because they do not want to make the same mistakes over and over. Third, human beings want to grow and progress. Knowing the good things that have happened in the past can help us set directions for the future.

Were There Historians in Ancient Greece?

Many people think that studying history is just something that we do today. But the ancient Greeks had excellent historians. The works of three of their greatest historians, Herodotus, Thucydides, and Xenophon, have been preserved for over two thousand years.

In their histories, Herodotus, Thucydides, and Xenophon did something very simple but very important: *they asked questions.* They did not begin from what they knew, but from what they wanted to find out. They tried to discover why things happened.

One day you may read what Herodotus wrote. If you do, you will think you are reading the notes of a traveller. As Herodotus travelled around Greece, he wrote about the sights, **customs**, and legends that interested him. He asked: "Why do the Greeks do this?" And he asked: "What were the causes and the outcomes of the war between Greece and Persia?" Then he found answers to his questions.

Thucydides wrote about why things happened. He described the causes and events of the Peloponnesian War between Athens and Sparta. Xenophon continued with Thucydides' work on the history of Greece.

If you read these histories of ancient Greece, you will also find out another thing. The historians thought that one subject was more important than all the others. That subject was war.

KEY FACTS

We would know very little about the influences of ancient Greece on Western civilization if it were not for the work of historians and archaeologists.

Modern historians still work like these early Greek historians worked. *They ask questions.* Then they try to answer their questions. The answers they find help us all to understand the ancient Greeks and ourselves a little bit better.

WHAT DO ARCHAEOLOGISTS DO?

Why do we know so much about the ancient Greeks? One answer is that archaeologists have told us. Archaeologists are scientists who dig up, or **excavate**, **artifacts** from the

Who Were Three Historians of Ancient Greece?

Herodotus (484-425 BC) wrote a book to try to explain and describe the Persian Wars. His history told what happened from about 700 BC to the defeat of the Persian king Xerxes in 479 BC. He called the book *History*.

Thucydides (460-400 BC) wrote about the Peloponnesian War (431-404 BC) between Sparta and Athens. He kept accurate records of the battles, but his work was never finished.

Xenophon (428-354 BC) wrote about the history of Greece from the point Thucydides' narrative breaks off.

• Herodotus was an ancient Greek historian who lived between 484 and 425 BC.
• Describe his approach to writing history.
• Can you name any famous modern historians?

• The historian Thucydides lived between 460 and 400 BC.
• Why do you think Thucydides and Herodotus both wrote about war?
• Why is it important to write about history?

remains of old civilizations. Then they study these artifacts to see how the people lived.

You may wonder why archaeologists have to "dig up" old civilizations. Did these civilizations live underground? The answer is that, after thousands of years, the blowing wind and shifting earth have covered these old civilizations. Layer after layer of dirt and sand may cover an ancient city that was once on top of the ground. Sometimes people from one city destroyed another city and then built a new one right on top of the ruins.

To find the remains of old civilizations, archaeologists must remove all the layers of dirt. Sometimes they can use large machinery to move the earth. At other times, when they know they are very close to a discovery, the only tools they can use are tiny brushes.

Archaeologists must be very careful they don't destroy anything important.

Many archaeologists have helped us find out about the ancient Greeks. One of these was Arthur Evans, who lived from 1851 to 1941. Evans was an English archaeologist who excavated the city of Knossos on Crete in 1899.

In his digging, Evans discovered the palace of Minos. In this palace were statues, paintings, and jewellery. Evans also found more than 4000 clay tablets. These tablets were marked with a form of ancient Greek writing. Some of this writing is so complex that we cannot interpret it, even today. Still, the artifacts that Evans dug up gave us many clues about how the Minoans and Mycenaeans lived.

• *Unearthing ancient treasures takes time and care.*
• *Why have iron bars been erected around this excavation site?*
• *What are some tools that archaeologists use?*

Heinrich Schliemann

Heinrich Schliemann was a German archaeologist who lived from 1822 to 1890. As a child, he learned the story of Troy from Homer's *Iliad* and *Odyssey*. Many people believed that the city of Troy and the Trojan Horse were nothing but fiction. But Schliemann believed there really was a Troy. Even as a child, he knew that when he grew up he would find it.

By the time he became an adult, Heinrich Schliemann was very wealthy. He spent some of his fortune and planned an expedition of discovery. In 1868, he set out to search for the legendary city of Troy.

To begin his search, Heinrich Schliemann asked the question: Where was Troy? To answer his question, he read the ancient poetry of Homer. Then he studied maps of the area Homer talked about in his poetry. When he went to that area and searched the land Homer had written about, he noticed a small hill. He guessed that this hill covered the city, and he began to dig.

Schliemann guessed right! Soon, he had uncovered not one city, but nine cities. Each city was built on top of the ruins of the last. By piecing the facts together and showing them to the world, Schliemann proved that Troy was more than a story. It had really existed.

But Heinrich Schliemann was not finished. In 1876, he discovered the circle of royal tombs at Mycenae. The treasure he found in the tombs proved that a great Greek civilization had existed a thousand years before Classical Greece. His discovery gave us a much clearer picture of the early years of ancient Greece.

WRAPPING UP

1. What is an artifact?
2. (a) What does a historian do?
   (b) What does an archaeologist do?
3. Herodotus, Thucydides, and Xenophon wrote about the reasons things happened. Herodotus asked the question: "Why do the Greeks do this?" Then, he answered his own question.
   (a) During a typical school day, think like a historian. Look around and ask: "Why does my school do this?"
   (b) List three questions you are curious about.
   (c) Now, try to find out the answers to these three questions.
   (d) Write what you find.
4. Historians and archaeologists find out about the past. However, they use different techniques to make their discoveries. How are the jobs of historians and archaeologists different? Are there any similarities? If so, what?
5. You have learned that archaeologists study artifacts of different cultures. You have also learned that an artifact can come from anywhere. It does not have to be dug up from under the ground. Pretend you are an archaeologist looking at artifacts in your home.
   (a) Choose a cupboard or a closet. Look at it with the eyes of an archaeologist.
   (b) List the things (artifacts) you find there.
   (c) Answer the following question: How does what you find there tell you about the culture of the people whose cupboard or closet it is?

6. Sometimes digging up artifacts can be controversial. Some explorers or scientists have dug up valuable treasures in their work. Some say, "I've done all the work. I should keep the treasure." But others say, "The discoveries belong to the world. They are too important to be kept by any one person." What do you think? Should discoveries belong to the individual who discovers them, or should they belong to the world and be put in a museum? Give reasons for your answer.

 ## DEVELOPING YOUR SKILLS

1. Watch an Indiana Jones movie (*Raiders of the Lost Ark* or *The Last Crusade*). Look at what the archaeologists do. List their activities. Do you think the movie is realistic about what these scientists do?
2. Talk with your parents and your grandparents. Write a brief history of your family.

 ## MOVING ON

In this chapter, you learned that historians and archaeologists give us clues about how ancient civilizations lived. You learned that the ancient Greeks left artifacts, and that by studying these artifacts you can see how civilizations changed over the years.

Did you know that you can learn more about ancient civilizations by studying things that have not changed much over time? For example, have you ever thought that when you look at the stars you may see a sky very similar to the one the Greeks saw 3000 years ago? What things about ancient Greece have not changed in thousands of years? Two answers are the geography and climate of the area.

The climate and geography of Greece have changed very little over time. As a result, the landscape and climate of Greece today help us understand why people made the choices they did in the past. In the next chapter, you will learn about ancient Greece by studying its geography and climate.

CHAPTER

4

The Geography and Climate of Ancient Greece

DIGGING UP

1. What are some ways the weather and land affect your daily life?

2 Greece is a rocky, mountainous place. It is a peninsula, surrounded on three sides by water. It also includes hundreds of islands. As you read this chapter, "dig up" several ways that climate and geography affected ancient Greek civilization.

WHAT DOES GREECE LOOK LIKE?

AS you saw in chapter 1, if you were to hunt for Greece on a map, you would look in southeastern Europe. There, extending into the Mediterranean Sea between Italy to the west and Turkey to the east, you would find Greece.

Much of Greece is a peninsula. It is surrounded on three sides by water. On the coastline of the Mediterranean and Aegean Seas, there are small areas of lowland. Inland there are very few **fertile** plains.

Greece also includes hundreds of small islands. These islands are scattered across the Ionian, Aegean, and Mediterranean Seas. The total land area of Greece is 131,957 square kilometres.

In chapter 1 of this book, you read that ancient Greece was one of the greatest civilizations in the world. It is now dead and gone. In its place, built right on top of the ruins of once-busy cities and homes, is a modern Greece. Modern Greece is a country not much different from any other European country.

Some things you will read about in this book have now disappeared. But many things mentioned in this book still exist. For example, if you visited Greece today, you could still see many remains of the buildings where the ancient Greeks lived and worshipped. These buildings may be ruins now, but they once were very busy and very important places during the Classical Period of Greece.

Relief Map of Greece

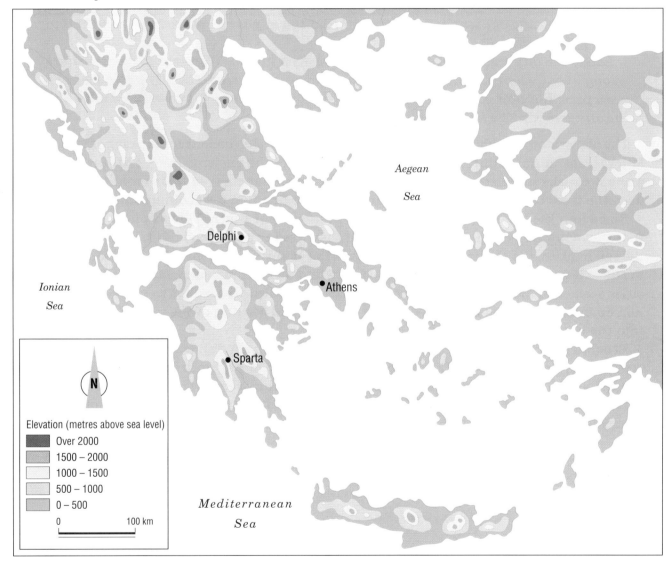

• *Greece has many mountains and valleys.*
• *Using the legend, tell how many metres above sea level Athens, Sparta, and Delphi are.*
• *Compare this map to the map on page 24. What does this map tell you about where the ancient city-states were located?*

THE CASE OF THE MISSING CITY

An archaeologist was once looking for an ancient city. He read many ancient stories about the city. From the stories, he learned that the city was located by the sea. After searching the coastline for many years, he could not find the ruins of the ancient city. The city had simply disappeared. He began to wonder why he could not find the city. Had the ancient stories been wrong? Had the city been covered by the sea? Had the city ever existed?

*Later, the city was discovered many kilometres inland. Were the ancient writers wrong about where the city had been? No, they were correct. The city had once been a sea **port**. But how could this be, if the city was found many kilometres inland? Had the city moved? The answer is quite simple.*

The above story is about an archaeologist looking for the ancient Ionian city of Miletus. Miletus was in Asia Minor, but was considered part of the ancient Greek civilization. The ancient Greeks in Miletus and Greece cut down trees that covered their mountains. They used the trees for building many things and to provide fuel for cooking and warmth.

Removing the trees did not seem important in ancient times. The people did not know that removing trees would damage the land they used to grow food. With no trees to hold the soil in place, the soil began to wash away. After many years, some of the harbours along the coast began to fill with the soil being washed into them from inland. Many ancient coastal cities seemed to move inland because their harbours filled with soil. The cities themselves had not really moved at all. The coastline had changed because of the soil being deposited into the harbours.

Erosion over thousands of years cannot be fixed easily. Today, some people worry that erosion can never be fixed. The ancient practice of cutting down trees has affected modern Greece. In many regions of the country, the best soil has been washed away or has been damaged. There might have been less damage to the soil if the people had known how important trees and forests are.

1. How did cutting the trees change the way people met their needs in ancient Greece?
2. What lesson can we learn about the importance of forests from the ancient Greeks?
3. Why is it important for us today to think about the way we treat our land, lakes, forests, oceans, and air?

The world has changed a great deal in 2000 years, but some things don't change. One thing that hasn't changed about Greece is its physical geography.

Greece has many mountains. In fact, most of mainland Greece is mountainous. These mountains are still in the same places they were thousands of years ago. They affect how the people of Greece live today, and how they lived in the past.

Around the mountains of Greece are many small valleys. The soil in these valleys is not always very fertile. Because of this, it has been difficult for the Greeks to grow crops.

One difference between modern and ancient Greece is the number of trees. In ancient Greece, trees covered the mountains. But the ancient people cut these trees and used them for buildings, boats, and fuel. After the trees were cut, there was little to hold back the water. Over the years, water washed away the best soil and deposited it on the seacoast. This washing-away process is called erosion.

• *The city of Trikkala in modern Greece is located in a valley surrounded by the Pindus mountains.*

• *Does this picture give you a clue as to why ancient Greek city-states were organized as they were?*

• *Was it easy for ancient Greeks to travel to different city-states? Explain your answer.*

 **KEY CONCEPTS** | **The environment and climate of an area affect how individual needs are met.**

How Does Geography Affect the Way People Live?

In any country, the geography affects how people live. Ancient Greece was no different. The geography of Greece made it hard for the Greeks to work together. Early Greek villages grew in the valleys between the mountains.

The valleys and mountain ranges separated these villages.

For most early civilizations, the easiest way to travel was on rivers. But, in Greece, there are few rivers large enough to travel on. The lack of rivers was another geographical feature that kept the ancient Greek city-states apart.

Because they could not work together, the people in these early Greek cities developed their own systems of government. They also developed their own cultures. They became individual Greek city-states. Though they were all Greek, each city-state had its own way of life.

 **KEY FACTS** | Greece has many mountains and very few large rivers. Unity between Greek city-states was difficult. Greek city-states developed in **isolation**.

 **KEY FACTS** — The early Greeks created city-states as a way to provide security from their enemies. The city-states also supplied goods for their people.

Greece is not a large country. No part of Greece is more than about 100 kilometres from a coastline, and islands make up one-fifth of all Greek land. As a result, Greece is a **maritime** nation. The ancient Greeks built ports on the mainland to help them ship goods from one place to another.

Ancient Greek City-States

• These were the main Greek city-states around 700 BC.
• Why do you think most of the city-states were close to a coastline?
• What do you think the climate would be like along the coastline? Explain your answer.

WHAT KIND OF CLIMATE DOES GREECE HAVE?

 **KEY FACTS** — The environment affects the food we can produce. The food the ancient Greeks produced depended on the climate and the fertility of their land.

Greece is a country of mountains and valleys. In the lowland valleys, the temperature is **moderate** year-round. Summers are long, hot, and dry. Summer skies are clear, with few clouds. In the winter, however, these valleys are rainy.

In the mountains, the climate is much cooler, and winters can be very cold. Summers in the mountains are very rainy. Frost and snow are uncommon in the valleys of Greece, but snow covers the mountains during the winter.

In Athens, the average summer temperature (July) is 31 degrees Celsius. In the winter (January), the average temperature is about 16 degrees Celsius.

The Mediterranean Sea affects the climate of Greece. Its climate is called a **Mediterranean climate**. Along the Greek coastline, the winds can blow very hard.

WRAPPING UP

1. Why did the Greek city-states develop independently of each other?
2. (a) Reread the section on the geography of Greece.
   (b) From your reading, pick five words or phrases that describe how Greece looks.
   (c) Compare what you have listed to the list of a classmate. Do you have a clear picture of the geography of Greece?
3. How would you describe the area in which you live? Write down five words or phrases that describe your geographical area. Compare these words or phrases with those of a classmate.
4. (a) How does your climate compare to the climate of Greece?
   (b) How does your climate affect the food you eat, the clothing you wear, or your lifestyle?
5. What does the climate have to do with what houses people build? Look up in another book some other geographical places with different climates. How do the houses reflect the differing climates?
6. Would your home meet the geographical or climatic needs of the people in ancient Greece? Why or why not?

DEVELOPING YOUR SKILLS

1. From the description of Greece given in the textbook, draw a series of pictures that show the Greek countryside. Place these pictures up in your class.
2. Using clues in the chapter, try to list other areas in the world that might have a similar climate or geography to Greece. What area closest to you has a similar geography or climate?

3. (a) Look at the map on page 24.
   (b) Using the scale on the map, find the distance in kilometres from:
   1) Athens to Sparta
   2) Delphi to Olympia
   3) Sparta to Argos
   4) Thebes to Corinth
   5) Corinth to Chalcis.
   (c) Look in a modern atlas and list which of these city-states still exist today. Give their latitudes and longitudes.

MOVING ON

In this chapter, you learned about the geography and climate of ancient Greece. You also learned that geography and climate shape how societies grow. You have already learned many things about ancient Greece, but there is still more for you to discover.

It is important to know that people have many of the same needs and desires. Once we realize this fact, we can begin another area of study. Here's a good question to begin your study: what do you need that all other people also need?

There are some simple answers to this question. All humans need to eat, drink, and rest to survive. These are basic needs. If we explore the lives of ancient people, we will find that they too had to meet these basic needs. But the ancient people did not always meet their basic needs in the same way we do.

In the next section, you will study how the ancient Greeks met their physical needs. Don't forget to note similarities and differences in your archaeological journal. Also, remember to use your historical and archaeological skills. It is helpful to remember when and where things happened.

PART II

Meeting Physical Needs

All human groups are different. But one thing you will learn as you study different civilizations is that all humans have the same types of needs. Sometimes one group of people is better at meeting its needs than other groups, and it becomes stronger than the others. Ancient Greece became a great civilization because the people were better at meeting their needs than other groups of people.

Human needs can be classified into three groups: (1) physical needs, (2) social needs, and (3) psychological needs. Physical needs can be defined as the needs that people have to take care of their physical body. Physical needs include needs like food, water, clothing, and shelter. Meeting these physical needs allowed the people in ancient Greece to live—to survive from one day to the next.

Like us, the Greeks had many physical needs. They needed food to eat. They needed water to drink. They needed clothing to protect themselves from the wind and the rain. And they needed homes to provide shelter. How the Greeks worked to satisfy their physical needs tells us much about their culture and civilization. The next chapter tells you some ways that the Greeks took care of their physical needs.

At Home in Ancient Greece

DIGGING UP

1. What are your favourite foods? Where does the food you eat come from? As you read this chapter, "dig up" one reason meat was a special food for people in ancient Greece.
2. We wear clothing to keep warm in winter and cool in summer. We also wear certain clothes because we like how we look in them. Which is most important to you? As you read this chapter, "dig up" some ways climate and fashion affected clothing in ancient Greece.
3. If you were building a home for yourself, what would it look like? What would some of its special features be? As you read this chapter, "dig up" some reasons many ancient Greek homes had courtyards.

WHAT DID THE ANCIENT GREEKS EAT?

WHAT did you eat last night for supper? You may have eaten a meal that contained some meat. If you eat a lot of meat, you eat very differently than the ancient Greeks. In ancient Greece, there was not enough suitable land to raise herds of cattle.

KEY CONCEPTS All people need food and water to meet their physical needs.

 **KEY FACTS**
> The ancient Greeks were limited in what they could produce for food because of the land and climate of their region.

The ancient Greeks ate very little meat. It wasn't that they disliked meat. On the contrary, meat was too special to eat every day. On special occasions, such as festivals or weddings, meals included meat. The ancient Greeks ate the meat and offered the fat and bones to the gods as a sacrifice.

People in ancient Greece ate many different foods. Their **staple** foods included olive oil, fish, goat cheese (feta), wine, and bread. Nuts and figs were considered **delicacies**. Vegetables included beans, peas, cabbage, onions, lettuce, lentils, and garlic. People in ancient Greece also ate poultry, eggs, small wild birds, fruit such as grapes, olives, honey, goat's milk, brains, barley porridge, pig's feet, black pudding (blood and fat), octopus, eel, lamb, and goat.

Ancient Greeks did not eat potatoes or rice. Why? Because they didn't know that these crops existed.

 **KEY FACTS**
> Ancient Greeks ate a variety of vegetables and little meat.

Most ancient Greeks, both young and old, drank wine. Wine was a staple drink of the culture, which doesn't mean that people in ancient Greece were **intoxicated**. Wine was always mixed with water to dilute it.

Ancient Greeks cooked their food either in the courtyard or on open **braziers** in the home. They heated soup, water, and vegetables in large jugs. They roasted meat in small clay ovens. There was no refrigeration in ancient

Greece, so the people couldn't save leftovers. Some leftovers were fed to the dogs.

Many families in ancient Greece had women slaves. These slaves helped prepare the family's meals and served the food to the family. They also helped with the housework. Slaves followed the instructions of the Greek wives.

Water is an important resource in any climate. In ancient Greece, where the climate was hot, fresh water was **scarce**. People got fresh water from the local well or they collected rain water at home. The local well was also a meeting place. Because of the scarcity of water, bathing was restricted. Ancient Greeks cleaned themselves with olive oil.

How Was Eating in Ancient Greece Different From Eating Today?

If you were suddenly transported back in time to a dinner in ancient Greece, you might not know what to eat your food with. The ancient Greeks did not use the same kind of cutlery we use today.

Food was cut into small pieces so that diners could eat it with their fingers.

Eating arrangements in ancient Greece were also different from today. Men ate while lying on couches. Women ate while sitting on chairs. On special occasions, diners wore wreaths while eating to honour the gods.

After-dinner parties were for men only. The men drank wine and discussed politics and business. It was also common to recite poetry or join in singing. Such an after-dinner party was called a **symposium**.

• *The people of ancient Greece ate a variety of foods. Like today, much of the daily activity of the ancient Greek home happened in the kitchen.*

• *Study the food in this ancient Greek kitchen. From what you have learned in health and science, would you say that people in ancient Greece had a good sense of nutrition? Why or why not?*

• *What familiar objects do you see in this kitchen? What did ancient Greek kitchens not have that we take for granted?*

What Was a Symposium?

In English, the word "symposium" means a group discussion. However, to the ancient Greeks, a symposium was an after-dinner party. If the host were wealthy, he paid for the meal and the party. If not, the guests paid for their share of the food, drink, and entertainment.

A symposium was very popular. Many people attended. Not everyone who came was invited. Often, people just heard there was a party and showed up. Friends were welcome at a symposium because the Greek host knew that each friend would host his own symposium as a repayment.

During the symposium, the guests drank wine diluted with water. They played games, danced, sang, and asked each other riddles. Sometimes the talk turned serious, about politics or matters of local concern for the city-state. Sometimes a symposium lasted until dawn.

The only women allowed at the symposium were entertainers. They played the flute or did acrobatic stunts.

• At a symposium, men ate and drank while lying down.
• What foods are in this picture? From your knowledge of agriculture in ancient Greece, what foods might have been served?
• Can you think of why women were usually excluded from a symposium?

WHAT DID THE ANCIENT GREEKS WEAR?

People in ancient Greece dressed differently than we do today. Ancient Greeks had different technologies for making clothing than we do today.

Ancient Greeks raised sheep. As a result, they wove much of their cloth from wool. By 500 BC, ancient Greeks also had linen to use for clothing. By the time of Alexander the Great, about 300 BC, cotton and silk were imported from the East.

You have learned that Greece has a Mediterranean climate. It is warmer than many areas of the world. Like all cultures, the ancient Greeks created clothing that suited their climate. For example, their clothes helped them live where it was warm. But the same clothes would not help people who live in a cold climate.

People in ancient Greece wore tunics called **chitons**. There were many different styles of chitons. Peasants wore short chitons because they needed to work. Chariot drivers wore longer chitons to protect them from the wind. Workers wore aprons so their chitons wouldn't wear out.

The Dorian chiton was made of a single piece of cloth. It was fastened on the shoulders and fell in folds. A belt was used to hold the open sides together.

The Ionian chiton had less material than the Dorian chiton. One side was sewn, and holes were cut for the head and arms. The Ionian chiton was made of linen, a lighter fabric than wool.

 **KEY FACTS**

Physical geography, climate, culture, and natural resources were all important in the types of clothes ancient Greeks made and wore.

 **KEY CONCEPTS**

Clothing meets our physical needs by protecting us from our environment. Clothing also reflects the beliefs and values of a society.

Where Did People in Ancient Greece Put Their Money?

Clothing has changed a great deal since the time of the ancient Greeks. One important bit of technology that we take for granted is the pocket.

Greek clothing didn't have pockets. Where did they keep their keys and money, you might ask. There were no keys to worry about in ancient Greece. Some people carried money in pouches or small purses attached to their belts. Occasionally, they would carry small coins in their cheeks. Today, we would be afraid of germs. But don't forget: the ancient Greeks didn't know that there were such things as germs.

What Was Fashionable in Ancient Greece?

Clothing serves many purposes. It covers and protects the human body. Through style and adornment, it also expresses status and taste. In ancient Greece clothing was both practical and decorative.

You may have seen drawings of ancient Greek women wearing white chitons. Actually, women's clothes were colourful. If you look closely at the statues from ancient Greece, you can see the remains of painted patterns on women's clothes. Red, yellow, and purple were the most popular colours. Fringes were added for decoration.

In ancient Greece, important men wore chitons that were bleached white. Other men wore chitons that were the natural colour of the wool.

KEY FACTS

In ancient Greece, everyone dressed differently. Men exercised and competed in athletic events in the nude. But it was not considered proper for women to do the same.

In chilly weather, people in ancient Greece wore a long cloak over their chiton. This cloak was called a **himation**. It was expensive. It was worn fastened by a brooch. A short cloak, called a **chlamys**, was popular among young people and warriors. When travelling, an ancient Greek wore a felt cap or a wide-brimmed felt hat called a **petasos**.

Ancient Greeks wore sandals in summer and high leather boots in winter. Some women wore sandals with several layers of undersoles so that they would appear taller.

• The ancient Greeks used clothing to protect themselves from the elements and to show social **status**.
• What can you tell about each person in the picture from the clothing they are wearing? What can you tell about the geography of Greece from the clothing?
• How did climate and geography affect the way the ancient Greeks dressed?

WHAT DID HOMES IN ANCIENT GREECE LOOK LIKE?

You have read about many similarities between the ancient Greeks and your society. In the area of housing, the people in ancient Greece had different values than we do. In ancient Greece, people built large and impressive marble temples to honour their gods and goddesses. Many ancient Greeks spent less time and attention on their homes than most of us do.

Homes in ancient Greece were not built as well as the temples and public buildings. Ancient Greeks thought it was more important to donate money to festivals or public buildings than to spend it on themselves. Most ancient Greeks were not interested in having large homes.

Some houses were built better than other houses. Some houses had stone foundations, thick mud brick walls, and heavy tiles on the roof. These homes lasted many years. However, only the foundations of these early homes can be seen today. The dampness and rain of thousands of years have washed the walls away.

Other homes in ancient Greece were not as sturdy. The thin mud brick walls broke easily because they were weakened by dampness and rain. Sometimes burglars — called "wall piercers" — could break through the weak walls. These homes fell apart as time passed, and nothing remains of them today.

Houses in ancient Greece could get very hot inside. The typical house in ancient Greece was built with an open courtyard in the centre. Families spent most of their time outdoors in the courtyard. Each courtyard had an altar. Sometimes it had a well for water. At other times, drains collected rain water in a courtyard pool.

Windows in ancient Greece had no panes of glass. Most windows faced the courtyard instead of the street. A window facing the street was an easy target for a thief. Also, since the sewers ran down the middle of the street, it was better to get fresh air from the courtyard rather than from the street.

Houses in ancient Greece also had a kitchen, a bathroom, a women's sitting room, a storeroom, and perhaps a slave's room. Some homes had two storeys. The upper storey had sleeping rooms. One of the largest rooms was the men's dining room. Women's quarters were at the rear of the house. Often the room next to the street was a shop. A home could include a potter's shop, a wine press, or an olive oil press.

The furniture in ancient Greece was simple. There were often three- or four-legged tables, couches, chairs, chests, woven rugs, and curtains. Utensils were hung on the walls because there were no shelves or cupboards. Houses were lit by lamps filled with olive oil. Even at the best of times, a Greek home was smoky.

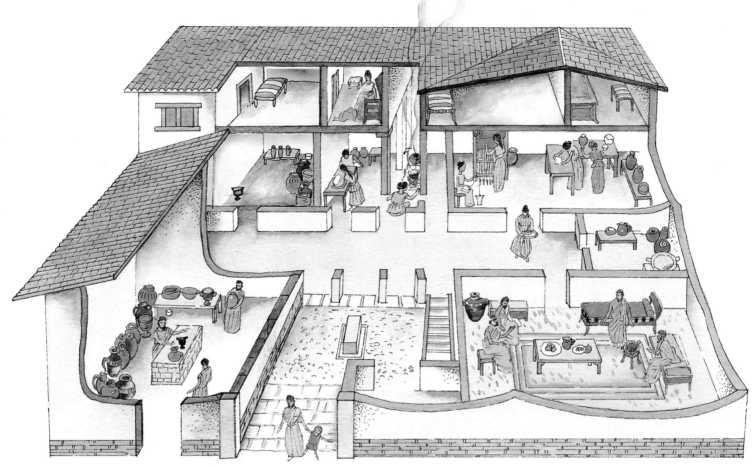

• A home in ancient Greece had many different rooms. Like our homes today, each room in an ancient Greek house had a particular purpose.
• How many rooms are in this home? Make a copy of this picture, and number and label each room you see in the picture. Make sure your label is based on what happens in that room.
• How were ancient Greek homes constructed? What were they made from?

Sometimes more than one family lived in a home in ancient Greece. A new bride would join her husband's family in their home. The new husband did not move in with his wife's family.

In ancient Greece, the saying "a man's home is his castle" was not true. Instead, "a woman's home was her castle," since the woman ran the home. Most men did not spend their time at home. They visited with other men, at their favourite meeting places. To some men in ancient Greece, their home was little more than a place to eat and sleep. To other men, their home was a very important place.

WRAPPING UP

1. Why are there few remains of ancient Greek homes?
2. How important were olives to the ancient Greeks? Look up olives in another source to help you with your answer.
3. What part of your home would be similar to the ancient Greek courtyard? Explain why.
4. List some differences between an Ionian chiton and a Dorian chiton.

5. Imagine that an ancient Greek has "time-travelled" and is now standing in your home! Make a list of objects or furnishings that would appear strange to him or her.

6. Think about the food that you typically eat and when you eat it. How are your climate and land related to the food you eat?

DEVELOPING YOUR SKILLS

1. We have learned much about the foods of the ancient Greeks. Do you think the foods you eat would be good for the ancient Greeks? What foods would you recommend to them? What foods would you not recommend? Do you think a fast-food restaurant would be a good thing to have in ancient Greece? Why or why not?

2. Combining ancient Greek chiton technology and today's fashions, draw a set of fashion chitons or a set of designer armour. Add designs to them that you might find in your school. Make sure you combine protection and fashion.

3. Draw the floor plan of your home and the floor plan of a home in ancient Greece. How are they similar? How are they different?

MOVING ON

In this chapter, you learned about the food and eating habits of the ancient Greeks. You learned that they ate food that was already in their environment. For example, the fish they ate came from the waters around them. You learned that they could grow some things, but not others, because the soil was not always fertile. You also learned that, like us, the ancient Greeks made choices. They did not use their scarce land for grazing herds of cattle.

You also learned about the clothing worn by ancient Greeks. You learned that this clothing helped the people survive in their climate. You discovered that men, women, and children dressed differently.

It may seem to you that things have changed very little. Clothing still provides protection. It also expresses differences in taste and status. Men, women, and children still dress differently. These are things we share with the ancient Greeks.

Ancient Greeks also shared our need for shelter. Some Greek homes had stone foundations and mud brick walls. There were many rooms within the house that served many purposes. The open courtyard in the centre of the home allowed families to spend time outside on hot days.

Is your study now over? Have you learned all there is to know about meeting our needs? Obviously, the answer is no. To learn more about a society, you must do more work.

As you look at your society, you will see that people have more than physical needs. There is also a group of needs that we have called social needs. Humans are social beings. We like to live together. Sometimes living together can cause problems. How can we solve these problems? That's one question we will study in the next section. We now begin to look at how the ancient Greeks worked to meet their social needs.

PART III

Meeting Social Needs

If a civilization is to survive, the people must be able to live with each other. Later, you will learn that the city-states of ancient Greece fought with each other until they were weak. Another civilization easily took over. The same thing could happen in any society.

As you have already read in this book, some groups of people are better at meeting their needs than other groups. The groups that are better at meeting their needs build **institutions** within their society. These institutions help them to remain friendly and polite, and to live in **harmony** with each other.

You have already read that all human groups are different. At the same time, all humans need to meet their social needs. People fulfill their social needs by living together in families, organizing governments and laws, speaking the same language, educating children, and defending themselves from danger.

Like us, the ancient Greeks had many social needs. We already learned that how the ancient Greeks satisfied their physical needs tells us much about their culture and civilization. This next part tells you some of the ways that the ancient Greeks took care of their social needs.

CHAPTER

Family Roles in Ancient Greece

DIGGING UP

1. How would you describe the roles of a mother or father in a family today?
2. As you read this chapter, "dig up" some of the differences between the roles of men and women in ancient Athens.
3. How did families in Athens differ from those in Sparta?

NOT all Greek city-states were the same. The two most important Greek city-states were Athens and Sparta. As you will read in this book, Athens was not at all like Sparta. In Athens, children were raised at home. Athenian women kept the houses and men lived with their families. In Sparta, children were brought up outside the home. Spartan women also did house-keeping chores. They had more slaves and servants to do their chores, and therefore had more freedom to pursue interests outside the home than women in Athens. Young men lived in army **barracks** until they married, and even after.

If you were magically transported in time back to Athens, you would find many things unfamiliar to you. However, you might feel more at home in ancient Athens than you would in ancient Sparta.

Where do men and women in your society spend their time? In ancient Greece, men and women lived differently from men and women today. Men believed it was important to spend time at meetings in the **agora**, barber shops,

• The agora was one of the busiest places in Greek city-states. Men attended meetings and women shopped for food every day at the agora.
• Compare the number of men and women in this picture. From what you have learned about ancient Greece, do you think this picture is accurate? Why or why not?
• The ancient Greeks did not have refrigeration. How did this affect their daily activities?

Ancient Greece Was a Sexist Society

A **sexist** society is one in which freedoms and duties are assigned because of a person's sex. Ancient Greece was a sexist society because the men and women who lived there were expected to follow certain roles based solely on their sex. For example, women did most of the daily grocery shopping. They also carried water from the public fountains to their homes. Women were not allowed to vote.

Can you name three roles that women had to do that men did not have to do in ancient Greece? Do you think people should be expected to follow certain roles based solely on their sex? Why or why not?

bathhouses, or blacksmiths. The people of ancient Athens felt that it was a sign of higher social status if the women did not have to go outside the home. For this reason, many women did most of their activities at home. Both men and women also attended festivals.

If your family has a party, what happens? In ancient Greece, women did not usually attend parties. Instead, they went to their quarters. At parties, the men drank wine, ate, and discussed philosophy.

It is important to understand that, in ancient Greece, people were treated differently. Men had greater status than women. Women had very different roles in their society than men had, but they did important things in the society. Slaves had the fewest rights of all, but were the backbone of the ancient Greek society.

HOW DID MEN IN ANCIENT ATHENS LIVE?

The people who lived in ancient Greece lived very differently from the way we live today. One difference was how men and women lived.

In ancient Athens, men and women shared very little time together outside their homes. Men spent their time with men. Women spent their time with women. Men spent most of their time outside the home doing business. Women spent most of their time in the home.

The more wealthy a family was, the more time men and women spent apart. In the homes of rich men in Athens, it was common for married men and women to live and sleep in separate rooms.

In North America, many men and women marry in their early to middle twenties. It was different in ancient Athens. In Athens, men didn't marry until they were in their thirties. The brides were often in their early teens.

- *Stone masons were members of the **middle class** in ancient Athens.*
- *What do you think the stone masons are doing in this picture?*
- *Think of ways that people in the middle class may have lived differently from the rich people and the poor people in ancient Greece.*

- ***Smiths** were artisans who made things out of metal.*
- *What can you tell about the lives of smiths by looking at this picture?*
- *Who were some other members of the ancient Greek middle class?*

In one way, the society of ancient Athens and today's society are very much alike. Jobs need to be done if the society is going to run smoothly. The difference was that, in ancient Athens, slaves did most of the manual work. You were considered poor if you did not have a slave. The ancient Athenians felt that having a slave was very important to their daily lives.

Wealthy men of ancient Athens were very busy. They went to city meetings. They acted as jurymen during trials. Or they visited with each other and discussed the problems of the day—from philosophy to business to city management. Rich fathers and mothers did little work with their hands. The only exception was that ancient Greek women did the **weaving** in the home. Weaving was considered a sign of social status.

Today, there are often big differences between how rich people live and how poor people live. In the middle, between the rich and the poor, is the middle class. Ancient Greece had a middle class too. Middle-class men worked very hard to make a living. Their work days lasted from sunrise to sunset. Many were artisans. They worked as carpenters, potters, metal smelters, shoemakers, blacksmiths, rope makers, sailors, and stone masons. They were farmers and small vendors. Their slaves helped with the manual work both in the home and in the workplace.

To meet the physical, social, and psychological needs of people, societies organize themselves into various groups. One important group is the family.

HOW DID MEN IN ANCIENT SPARTA LIVE?

Look up the word *spartan* in the dictionary and write down what it means. The word spartan comes from the way the people of Sparta lived. The definition tells us a bit about life in Sparta.

In Sparta, life was more like a military camp than a home. Men lived together in barracks. Why? So they could come to think and act the same. The Spartans stressed military discipline. Spartan men were interested in the life of a soldier. For the Spartans, the military "team" was more important than the family. Love of Sparta was encouraged even over the love of the family.

Spartan men were allowed to be married. But if they wanted to visit their families they had to sneak away from their camps and return in time to perform their duties and exercises. The purpose of marriage in Sparta, as it is in many societies, was to have more children. The Spartans believed that the strength of their city-state depended on a growing population.

HOW DID WOMEN IN ANCIENT ATHENS LIVE?

You have already learned some things about women in ancient Athens. You have learned that women had different roles from men in that society.

• Most women in ancient Athens took care of the family and the household.
• By looking at things in the picture, what can you tell about life in ancient Greece?
• In this picture, the baby is sitting in a kind of chair. What two purposes did this chair probably have?

In ancient Athens, women had few **civic** rights or responsibilities. Mostly, they stayed in the home, where they managed the household. The men were away from home most of the time. Women of Athens could not vote, attend meetings or the Olympics, or act on stage. Men did these activities, including playing women's parts in dramas. Some women did work outside the home, usually in the markets of Athens.

In ancient Athens, most families had at least one slave to help with the household chores. The women usually supervised all the work of the home, except for the weaving. They did the weaving themselves.

Household tasks included grinding grain into flour, fetching water from public fountain houses, cooking, weaving, and cleaning the home. Remember, there was no refrigeration and no electricity. Every meal every day was an event. It took a long time to get each meal ready.

The idea that women should not be outside the home unless they were escorted was supported by the entire society. Most women in ancient Greece did not have the same advantages as men had. But it would be wrong to believe that women were not important in ancient Greek society. Some Greek women became active outside their homes. Two examples of women who became important in Greek society are Sappho and Aspasia.

As you learned earlier in this chapter, the men of ancient Athens usually didn't marry until they were in their thirties. The women usually married by the time they were 15. Athenian men and women did not choose their husbands. Instead, fathers arranged the marriages of both their sons and their daughters.

• *This ancient Greek woman is cooking a meal for her family.*
• *What can you tell about ancient Greek cooking methods from this picture?*
• *Explain why meals took a long time to prepare in ancient Greece.*

Two Famous Women of Ancient Greece

Sappho

Sappho is one of the most famous women of ancient Greece. She lived about 610-565 BC. She wrote nine books of lyric poems, and invented the **plectrum** (for striking the lyre). She also wrote many different kinds of poetry and solo songs.

Sappho was born on the island of Lesbos in the city of Mytilene. She was married to a very wealthy man, a trader from Andros. She had one daughter whom she named after her mother, Cleis.

Over the centuries, many people have been fascinated by Sappho. In fact, dozens of stories have been written about her. Because her poetry did not reveal much about her life, people read her poetry and try to guess what she was like.

Sappho's poems express human feelings. Many reflect how she felt about her life. In one of her poems she wrote about her love for her daughter, Cleis. One line stated: "I have a beautiful child who looks like golden flowers, my darling Cleis, for whom I would not (take) all Lydia...."

• *Sappho is one of the most famous women of ancient Greece.*
• *How was Sappho's life different from the lives of other ancient Greek women? How was her life the same?*
• *Can we learn anything about history by reading poetry?*

Aspasia

Aspasia is one of ancient Athens' most famous women. Except for Sappho, she may be the most famous woman in all of ancient Greek history. One historian has said, "She added a sparkle of her own to the city's Golden Age."

Aspasia was born in the Ionian city of Miletus in Asia Minor. She was the daughter of a **citizen** named Axiochus. At an early age, for some unknown reason, Aspasia lost her freedom and was sold as a slave.

Although she was a slave, Aspasia received a high-quality education, which other women of the day did not receive. She was trained in philosophy, history, politics, science, art, and literature. Her education helped her become influential.

Aspasia was a brilliant thinker. She was also known for her ability in public speaking and her leadership. During her life, she became a close friend to Pericles, a general of great power and position in Athens. Some men thought she influenced too many of Pericles' decisions. Many resented her power. One ancient writer accused her of starting a war with Samos in 441 BC because her home, Miletus, was involved in a dispute with the island.

It is not known when Aspasia died. Very little is known of her after Pericles died. Today, we recognize Aspasia for her rise to fame as one of the most influential and powerful women in ancient Greece. In a world controlled by men, this was truly an accomplishment.

What Was a Wedding Like in Ancient Athens?

Weddings in ancient Athens were not like those of today. The bride and groom did not sign a register. The marriage was a private contract. It was considered legal from the moment the woman entered the man's home.

Before she was married, the young woman took her dolls to a nearby temple as an offering to the goddess Artemis. She then took a ritual bath.

The wedding took place at the woman's home. There was a feast and a ceremony, and the young, veiled bride went with her new husband and the best man to the new husband's home. At the new home, the young woman accepted the task of running the household and having her husband's children.

Gifts presented at a wedding party helped the new couple furnish their home. Housewarming presents were also given to the couple one day after the wedding. Two days after the wedding, the bride appeared for the first time — unveiled.

• *These statues show Spartan women running. Spartan women were more active than the women of Athens.*
• *What differences do you see between these women and the Athenian woman shown on page 41?*
• *How were Spartan girls raised differently from girls in Athens?*

HOW DID WOMEN IN ANCIENT SPARTA LIVE?

The women of Sparta lived very differently from the women of Athens. In Sparta, men lived in barracks. Women were freer to leave the home. Although they could not vote or hold office, many important decisions were made by Spartan women about their homes and even their communities. Unlike women in Athens, Spartan women had economic power.

Men and women in Sparta were more equal in many ways than they were in ancient Athens. Spartan girls learned many of the same physical skills that boys learned. Ancient Spartans honoured bravery and courage in men and women. Spartan mothers expected their sons to be brave. They told their sons, the young Spartan soldiers: "Come back with your shield, or on it!" (In ancient Greece, a dead or wounded soldier was carried on his shield. The shield acted as both a piece of armour and as a stretcher.)

HOW DID CHILDREN IN ANCIENT ATHENS LIVE?

Children in ancient Athens were taught to be obedient always. Sons of wealthy men went to school at age six or seven. The purpose of school was to train both the mind and the body. Girls were taught at home. Here they learned the skills they would need to manage the household.

In ancient Athens, children were treated well. Most children had many toys to play with. Children also had many pets. They played with dogs, ducks, mice, and even grasshoppers.

Remember that societies are different. What seems right in one society often seems wrong in another. We owe a great debt to the people of ancient Athens. Still, many of the things that the people of ancient Athens did seem strange, and even cruel, to us.

One of the hardest things to understand about ancient Greece was how people treated babies. In Athens, the baby's father could decide whether it lived or died. Babies were often left on the steps of a temple or on the street where someone passing by could take it. Sometimes the baby was given away and became a slave in another household.

Why did the people of ancient Athens do this? Perhaps the baby was weak or sickly. Perhaps the family might not have been able to feed one more child. Sometimes babies were not wanted.

HOW DID CHILDREN IN ANCIENT SPARTA LIVE?

People in ancient Sparta may seem even more cruel to us. At birth, all babies were inspected by officers who worked for the city-state. These officers decided if a baby would live or die. A healthy baby could live. The rest were left to die, usually on a mountainside.

Children in ancient Sparta were treated harshly. They were not allowed to cry, be afraid of the dark, or throw temper tantrums.

At the age of seven, boys went to live in military barracks. Here they were trained to be good Spartans. They were taught the skills needed to survive as a soldier. They learned to lie, steal, and **forage** for food so they would not starve.

Girls in ancient Sparta were more **liberated** than girls of other city-states. They could leave their homes. They were brought up to be independent and were given the chance to own land. They enjoyed freedoms that ancient Athenian women did not have.

 **KEY FACTS**

To meet their physical, social, and psychological needs the ancient Greeks developed specific roles for each family member. These roles (things expected from you) were based on the values of the society. In ancient Greece, men, women, and children had different roles.

 **KEY FACTS**

Throughout history, the family has been important in every society. Each Greek city-state had its own family organization. Spartan families were very different from Athenian families.

• *In Sparta, mothers encouraged their sons to fight bravely.*
• *This Spartan soldier does not have all of his equipment. What equipment does he have? List the pieces. Then, list how each piece might have been used.*
• *What training would this young Spartan have had before going into battle?*

WRAPPING UP

1. What happened to unwanted babies in ancient Sparta?
2. In your own words, describe an ancient Greek wedding.
3. (a) Have you been to a wedding? If you have, write a description about what happens at a modern wedding. Why do you think things happen as they do? If you have not been to a wedding, talk with someone who has.
   (b) Compare a wedding in ancient Greece with a modern wedding. What are the similarities and differences?
4. One of the key points in this chapter is that men dominated ancient Greek society and women had few rights.

Review the chapter. List points from the chapter that would support this point.

5 (a) How is your life different from that of a child in ancient Greece?

(b) In what ways are the lives of women today different from those of ancient Greek city-states?

6. (a) Would you rather be a child in ancient Athens or Sparta? Why?

(b) Would you rather be a boy or a girl in ancient Greek society? Why?

DEVELOPING YOUR SKILLS

1. Research the history of toys. Compare the earliest toys, including those used in ancient Greece, with the kind of toys young people today play with. Have the kinds and types of toys changed throughout history? Has the idea of play changed throughout history?

2. Design a word search on Family Roles using vocabulary from this chapter.

3. Use the following chart to show the difference between life in ancient Athens and ancient Sparta. The purpose of the chart is to compare how men, women, and children lived in the different city-states. On your chart make sure to write your information briefly, but completely. (You may use information from other chapters, if you need to.)

MOVING ON

In this chapter, you learned that the family helped the ancient Greeks meet their social needs. You learned that in ancient Greece family members had roles that were both similar to and different from those of families today. You discovered that most Greek women stayed home with their children, while men travelled and met with others. You also learned something about Greek children. They played, they learned many things, and sometimes they worked in their homes.

In the next chapter, you will learn about what kinds of occupations people in ancient Greece had.

MEN		WOMEN		CHILDREN	
Athens	Sparta	Athens	Sparta	Athens	Sparta

SAMPLE CHART

Occupations in Ancient Greece

DIGGING UP

1. What would you like to be when you grow up? Give some reasons you would choose this occupation.
2. If you lived in ancient Greece, what occupation would you prefer to have? As you read this chapter, "dig up" some reasons for your choice.

IF a civilization is to grow, its people must be active and working. One reason you study ancient Greece in school is because the ancient Greeks were active and working people. The things they created have lasted a long time.

In ancient Greece, work was a way that people met their own needs and the needs of others.

 **KEY CONCEPTS**

A society meets social and physical needs by creating work for its people. Work allows people to act together to meet each other's needs.

 **KEY FACTS** | Ancient Greek society was organized into different occupations. These occupations helped the Greeks meet their physical and social needs.

HOW DID FARMERS CONTRIBUTE TO SOCIETY IN ANCIENT GREECE?

Agriculture is very important in any society. Without farmers, there would be no food. Without food, people could not live.

Although the soil of Greece is not always fertile, Greece has many farmers. Farmers in ancient Greece probably lived differently from farmers where you live. In ancient Greece, many farmers lived in villages or small hamlets, not on their farms. Every morning they woke early to walk or ride to their farms. Every evening they returned to their homes.

Ancient Greece was a slave society. On Greek farms, slaves and farmers worked together. However, the slaves did the hardest work.

Farms in ancient Greece were small. Land for farming was scarce. In poor soil, the ancient Greeks planted a crop that would grow. The crop was olives. Olives were the most important crop in ancient Greece.

• *Olives are still an important crop in Greece.*
• *Why were olive trees essential to the ancient Greeks?*
• *Think of ways that you use olive products in your daily life.*

How Important Were Olive Trees to Ancient Greece?

Ancient Greeks used olives and olive oil in many different ways. Olive oil was used in cooking and eating, and for lamp fuel. One of its most important uses was for cleaning. After washing themselves, men rubbed their skin with olive oil. Women rubbed perfumed oil on themselves. People sometimes bathed with a highly scented soap made with olive oil and **alkaline** materials. People who did not have a bathtub scrubbed their bodies with olive oil.

Olive trees had one major disadvantage. They took a long time to grow and mature. Enemies of the ancient Greeks knew how important these olive trees were to the Greek people. Attacking olive trees was less dangerous than fighting Greek soldiers, but just as harmful. If an enemy could destroy the olive trees, it could disrupt the Greek way of life. Of course, destroying the olive trees was not considered honourable and was rarely done.

Because there was little flat land in Greece, even the hilly ground was planted. To allow crops to grow, the sides of hills were **terraced**. These terraces provided more land for planting crops. Ploughs were pulled by mules or oxen.

• *Ancient Greeks terraced their hillsides to provide more room to grow crops.*
• *Look at the picture and describe what terracing is.*
• *Try to explain how terracing gave Greek farmers more land to plant crops.*

Where the soil was fertile, the ancient Greeks grew grain and vegetables. Bread was a staple food. Crops and vegetables included wheat, barley, chickpeas, beans, turnips, onions, and garlic.

Another important crop was grapes. Grapes were grown to eat fresh and as raisins, and also for wine.

 **KEY CONCEPTS**

The environment of a country forces people to work together in order to survive.

In ancient Greece, farmers kept sheep and sometimes pigs for meat. Because fodder for the animals was rare, the herds were kept small. Extra animals were slaughtered in the spring. Spring was a time for feasting in ancient Greece.

Sheep also provided wool for cloth. Goats provided milk and cheese.

What Is a Good Farmer?

Hesiod was a poet who lived in Boeotia in about 700 BC. In *Works and Days*, Hesiod offered some practical advice to his brother, a farmer. Hesiod gave rules for the just farmer. Here is his advice:

1. Don't marry early.
2. Work hard even in winter.
3. Make sacrifices to the gods.
4. Be friendly with your neighbours.
5. Never lend or borrow anything.
6. Avoid unlucky days.
7. Have only one son.

Did Ancient Greeks Have a "Sweet Tooth"?

The ancient Greeks grew many important foods. However, there were some crops that could not be grown. As you look at the list of the crops grown in ancient Greece, what important crops are missing? What crops aren't grown that you use every day? Probably the most obvious answer is sugar.

Where did the ancient Greeks get sugar? Did they even have sugar to use? If they didn't have sugar, how did they sweeten their food? The answer is that the Greeks did not have sugar. They used honey to sweeten their food. Because honey was their only "sugar," raising honeybees became an important occupation in ancient Greece.

How do you think the first human to eat honey thought to do it or dared to try?

Months of the Year

Athenian months of the year were lunar months. In the following list, the Greek spellings are used.

Hekatombaion	June - July
Metageitnion	July - August
Boedromion	August - September
Pyanepsion	September - October
Maimakterion	October - November
Poseideion	November - December
Gamelion	December - January
Anthesterion	January - February
Elaphebolion	February - March
Mounikhion	March - April
Thargelion	April - May
Skirophorion	May - June

What Did Ancient Greek Farmers Do at Different Seasons?

For the ancient Greeks, there was an activity for each season of the year. For example, in Gamelion, farmers pruned their vines. They pulled weeds and picked insects off plants in Elaphebolion. In Metageitnion, they picked their grapes, spread them out for 10 days in the sun, then pressed them into wine.

Farmers shook olives from the trees in Boedromion. They planted wheat in Pyanepsion and harvested it in Mounikhion. For every activity, there was a season.

HOW DID ARTISANS CONTRIBUTE TO SOCIETY IN ANCIENT GREECE?

Ancient Greece had a thriving group of artisans. These artisans made the tools that the people needed for their work. These tools included carts, ploughs, and fishing nets.

Two important jobs in ancient Greece were metal-working and tanning. Smiths shaped raw metal ores into useful products. In an advanced society such as ancient Greece, metals were important. They were used in coins, ploughs, tools, works of art, and weapons. Iron smiths **smelted** iron to make tools and weapons. Bronze workers cast and polished beautiful statues.

Tanners turned the hides of animals into leather. Leather was used for armour, clothing, tools, and sandals. Leather was useful because it could be shaped into straps to hold things in place. Preparing an animal hide for leather took two steps. First, the hide had to be scraped. Second, the hide had to be **cured.** Tanners used strong, smelly acids to take the hair, dirt, and meat off the skin.

 **KEY FACTS**
Ancient Greek artisans contributed greatly to their society. They provided services, tools, and instruments to make life easier for the people. They left us many artifacts to study.

HOW DID POTTERS CONTRIBUTE TO SOCIETY IN ANCIENT GREECE?

In ancient Greek society, potters were important artisans. Today, most pottery is created by artists. The pottery they produce is more for decoration than for storing or carrying food or water. But in ancient Greece, clay pottery had many uses. Potters made pots, jars, vases, cups, toys, tiles, lamps, braziers, and bowls. There were no plastic, glass, or paper containers in ancient Greece. Some pots and **utensils** were made from clay by a potter. Bronze was also used for some pots and utensils.

Ancient Greek pottery is still useful. Modern archaeologists can tell much about Greek culture and society by studying pottery. First, the shape of pottery tells us how it was used. Second, and maybe more important, artists painted on their pottery scenes of everyday life. Much of what we have learned about Greek civilization is based on these scenes. Third, the style of pottery helps archaeologists identify how old the pottery is.

A great deal of skill was needed for making good pottery. Pots were worked by hand or on a potter's wheel. After they were shaped, they were dried in the sun, polished, painted, and baked in an outdoor kiln.

Potters used a special black paint, which made the pottery beautiful and strong. Athenian pots were highly prized for their beautiful decoration.

Today, ancient Greek pots can be found all over the Mediterranean world. The Greeks **exported** them to other countries, usually filled with olive oil.

 **KEY FACTS**

Greek potters supplied the vessels their society used to carry and store food and water.

The Two Styles of Greek Pots

Greek pottery was usually designed in two ways. One design was a pot with figures painted in black over the natural red clay. The style was very basic. A more **intricate** design was to leave the figures and scenes in red and cover the rest of the pot with black paint.

HOW DID SCULPTORS CONTRIBUTE TO SOCIETY IN ANCIENT GREECE?

If you visited Athens today, you would be able to tell how important sculptors were to ancient Greece. Using a few simple tools such as drills, chisels, and **punches,** sculptors in

 **KEY FACTS**

Ancient Greek sculptors created designs in marble. Because marble does not wear down easily, many of their sculptures exist today.

ancient Greece created designs on rock-hard marble. Because the marble is so hard, it has lasted for centuries. It promises to last much longer.

Sculptors in ancient Greece used marble and other kinds of stone to create statues of their gods and goddesses. The statues carved out of marble were then painted. Sometimes these statues were life-sized. Sometimes these statues were gigantic. For example, the statue of Athena in the Parthenon was more than 12 metres tall. Some sculptures weighed so much that it took hundreds of people to move them.

• Potters painted scenes of ancient Greek life on their vases.
• This vase shows Olympic events. Try to name some of the events.
• How were vases produced in ancient Greece?

Even when creating statues, the ancient Greeks treated men and women differently. Female statues were almost always clothed. Male statues were often naked.

The most famous sculptor of ancient Greece was Pheidias. He directed the work on the Parthenon in Athens.

CASE
STUDY

HOW HAS ACID RAIN HARMED STATUES?

Sculptors created statues that were made to last. In ancient Greece, statues were carved from marble. Working with rock as hard as marble took extra time, but to the ancient Greeks the extra work was worth it. Marble is so hard that it erodes very slowly. The ancient Greeks wanted their work to live on, even after they died.

Statues from ancient Greece have lasted for centuries. Some buildings have been partly destroyed by wars and other disasters. If you were to touch the statues and buildings, you would notice that many have been worn down, almost as if someone has rubbed them with sandpaper. Over a thousand years of rain and wind have slowly worn down the stone structures.

The rain and wind were expected. But sculptors in ancient Greece did not know that a society far in the future would create a substance powerful enough to crumble even marble. The substance is **acid rain.**

Some experts say that acid rain has done more damage to statues and buildings in the last few years than centuries of rain, wind, and storms. In less than 50 years, acid rain has begun to wear away the noses and ears of some statues. The faces and arms have worn off others. Without protection and preservation, entire statues may soon fall apart.

Acid rain is powerful pollution. It kills vegetation, fish, and wildlife. It can rust the outside surfaces of buildings and other structures. The ancient ruins of great civilizations may soon be destroyed by the effects of acid rain.

Acid rain is a serious problem. It is important that we find some way to stop the damage it causes. It is a special problem to modern-day Greeks who want to preserve the sculptures of their ancestors. They are trying to protect their statues, but the job is difficult.

1. What damage has acid rain done to some ancient Greek structures?
2. In another resource book, look up the causes of acid rain.
   (a) Make a list of the causes of acid rain.
   (b) What ways might we reduce acid rain?
3. Why is it important to find a way to limit the damage caused by acid rain?

KEY FACTS

Societies soon learn to use their natural resources to feed themselves. The waters around ancient Greece were full of fish. The people soon learned to use fish for food.

HOW DID FISHING CONTRIBUTE TO SOCIETY IN ANCIENT GREECE?

The water around the city-states of ancient Greece teemed with fish. These fish provided an important source of food for the people. One of the most important jobs in ancient Greek society was the job of fishing.

The long coastline and many islands of Greece made fishing a natural choice for an occupation. Many people on the coast were involved in fishing.

Some people fished close to shore, using small boats and nets. Other people used stationary nets that were set in shallow coastal waters. They did not need a boat for this method of fishing. Other people used a line and gorge to catch fish. A gorge was a small stick with two sharp ends covered with bait. This type of fishing was usually done to catch fish for one's own use and not to sell at the market.

HOW DID DOCTORS CONTRIBUTE TO SOCIETY IN ANCIENT GREECE?

The ancient Greeks did not know as much about medicine and health as doctors know today. But doctors in ancient Greece were not ignorant about the human body.

The most famous Greek doctor was Hippocrates. Hippocrates had a great influence on the medicine of the day. Before Hippocrates, most attempts to heal were based on superstition, not on fact. Hippocrates studied the human body carefully. His studies helped provide guidelines for surgery. The Hippocratic Oath was named after Hippocrates and his teachings. For his tremendous contributions, Hippocrates is known as the "father of medicine."

Hippocrates

Hippocrates (469-399 BC) kept careful records of medical cases. He discovered many useful drugs. Doctors today must recite the Hippocratic Oath, in which they swear never to cause harm to a patient. Hippocrates did not actually compose the oath, although his teachings agree with it.

• *Hippocrates has greatly influenced how doctors practise medicine.*
• *What were some of Hippocrates' ideas?*
• *Find out more about the Hippocratic Oath. What role does this oath play in medicine today?*

When doctors carefully observe the symptoms of a disease before they prescribe treatment or medicine, they are using the ideas of Hippocrates.

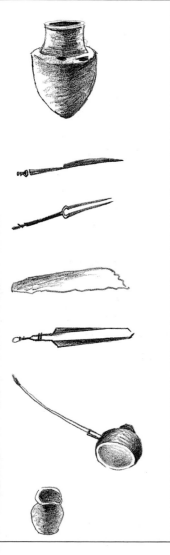

• *Doctors in ancient Greece used many different medical instruments.*

• *Can you identify the medical instruments in this picture? What do you think each medical instrument might be used for?*

• *What medical techniques did doctors in ancient Greece perform?*

Doctors in ancient Greece had a simple diagnosis for disease. Most diseases, they believed, were caused by the patient's elements being out of balance. The elements, or humours, were blood, phlegm, yellow bile, and black bile. The treatment? Get the body back in balance. Usually, Greek doctors prescribed a simple treatment: rest, proper diet, and exercise. It would be difficult to fault this prescription for a healthy life.

Doctors in the ancient world had ideas we probably would consider strange. Patients were often **bled** to remove the "bad blood" that made them ill. Doctors did not understand how the internal organs or blood circulation worked. These early doctors were good surgeons. However, most successful surgery was external, not internal.

When ancient Greeks became sick, they would often visit the shrine of Asclepius. Here they would ask the gods to cure them. The shrine of Asclepius was the ancient Greek version of our hospital. The priests were trained doctors.

WHAT WERE SOME OTHER OCCUPATIONS IN ANCIENT GREECE?

Barbershops were a favourite meeting place for men of ancient Greece, and barbers did a great business. Other occupations in ancient Greece included a cook at the agora, a houseboy, a chariot driver, and a field hand.

People in ancient Greece met their social needs by doing many different jobs. Each job helped build the society. Though some jobs may have appeared more important than others, remember that every job helps build a great civilization.

Carpenters were important in Greek society. These carpenters built tables, chairs, and other furniture. They learned how to steam wood so it could be bent. They used a machine called a **lathe** to **turn** a piece of wood to make legs for tables and chairs. Unfortunately, wood rots quickly. On vases we have drawings of ancient Greek tables, but there is no real furniture left for us to see.

WRAPPING UP

1. What were the most important occupations in ancient Greek society? Why?
2. Choose three of the occupations mentioned in this chapter that you find most interesting. Describe these occupations in your own words.
3. How would it feel to work as an iron smith, tanner, or potter in ancient Greece? Which would you rather do? Why?
4. How are these occupations similar or different from the work people do today? Are there any occupations mentioned that still are important? Why have some occupations disappeared?
5. If an ancient Greek were to come to your country, what occupations would seem familiar to him or her? Name a few that would be difficult for the person to understand.
6. (a) What job would you have liked to do in ancient Greece? What training would you have needed?
   (b) If you were to travel back in time, what do you know that would help the ancient Greeks the most?

DEVELOPING YOUR SKILLS

1. Using red construction paper, create
   (a) your own "ancient Greek" vase. Be sure to show everyday scenes of your life for future generations to find. (You might use a black felt pen for the design) OR
   (b) draw figures in black felt pen on red paper but do not fill them in (leave red). Colour or paint the rest of the paper black.
2. Draw a picture of a vase. On the vase, create a scene that would describe something about your daily life. Pretend you are an archaeologist and write a short report about what you have learned about your culture. Be prepared to share your find with the rest of the class.

MOVING ON

In this chapter, you learned that the ancient Greeks worked at many important jobs. These jobs provided the food, clothing, tools, and weapons that the people needed to grow and prosper. These jobs also gave the people an income so they could buy things from each other.

In the next chapter, you will learn about the role of slaves in ancient Greece.

Slaves in Ancient Greece

DIGGING UP

1. Write a definition of slavery. Why do you think slavery is seen as unacceptable today?
2. As you read this chapter, "dig up" some differences between slaves in ancient Athens and in ancient Sparta.

WHY DID THE ANCIENT GREEKS HAVE SLAVES?

THE society of ancient Greece differed from modern society in one important way. Ancient Greece was a slave society. Most families that could afford slaves had them.

When we read about the ancient Greeks, it is important to remember that they took men and women and held them against their will. Slaves were real people, just like we are.

But to the ancient Greeks, slaves were things, not people. To the ancient Greeks, slavery was acceptable. Owning slaves was natural. Slaves were important to the ancient Greeks. Slaves did much of the work of the city-state.

• *Slaves were bought and sold at marketplaces throughout ancient Greece.*
• *In this drawing, what does the artist do to show her feelings about the slave sale? What do you think her feelings are? Give reasons for your answers.*
• *Can you name other societies throughout history that have had slaves?*

Today, slavery is unlawful. We believe that all men and women should have equal rights. Many people wonder how a society could use slaves. People today believe it is morally wrong to own human beings or keep them as slaves.

Historians of today believe that almost one-third of the population of ancient Greece were slaves. Most city-states had many slaves. Wealthy people in ancient Greece had many slaves. Most families had at least one slave.

Being a family slave was the easiest. Most slave owners treated the slaves quite well. Family slaves worked as cooks, porters, **paedogogos** (a guardian slave who took the children to school), houseworkers, gardeners, and secretaries. Slaves were expected to be faithful to the family.

Other slaves, like those working in the silver mines of ancient Athens, led terrible lives. Many died of exhaustion. The most common occupations for ancient slaves were in the mines. Working in mines was one job that the ancient Greek citizen did not do. Slaves also worked on farms and in workshops. They worked as skilled workers and entertainers. Many female slaves were trained as singers and dancers.

Slaves of ancient Greece sometimes worked side by side with their owners. As you read earlier, on Greek farms, slaves and farmers worked together.

Slaves in ancient Greece were considered property, not human beings. They could be given away or inherited. They could be bought or sold like any other piece of property.

Most slaves who came to ancient Greece were prisoners of war. Their captors would bring the slaves to a port such as Athens and sell them there. In some cases, children were sold by their parents because the family was too poor to care for them.

Once a person was a slave, it was difficult to become a free person. Children of slaves were also slaves. They became the property of their parents' owners. Slaves could be freed by their owners, or they could buy their freedom by earning enough money.

As in the rest of society, there were differences between slaves in ancient Athens and in ancient Sparta. The main difference was that Athenian slaves had been uprooted from their families and conquered country. Spartan slaves were **serfs** who lived in the same place as their ancestors.

How Much Did a Slave Cost in Ancient Athens?

Remember that slaves were people, just like you. But in ancient Greece, slaves were considered property. Their value depended on how useful they were to the family or workplace. The common rate of pay in Classical Athens was one drachma per day. If you take $70 as a typical daily rate for a skilled labourer today, you see that slaves were expensive.

Here are some average prices for a slave, both in ancient Greek money and in today's dollars.

Skilled slave (a mine foreman) = 6000 drachmas, or $420,000

Mine worker = 150 drachmas, or $10,500

Artisan (sword smith) = 300 drachmas, or $21,000

House slave = 170 drachmas, or $11,900

 KEY CONCEPTS   **Many civilizations have depended on slavery to meet their social, physical, and psychological needs. Slaves provided a huge labour force. Slavery allowed ancient Greek city-states to meet their needs and to prosper.**

In Sparta, the slaves were called **Helots.** Helots were more like tenant farmers. They were bound to the land they cultivated for Spartan owners. They were "free" in the sense that they could not be sold, could own personal property, and could marry other Helots.

Helots outnumbered Spartans. As Spartan boys grew up, they were taught to go hunting at night for Helots found out of doors. If they found a Helot outside, they would immediately kill the slave. Because they were treated badly, most slaves in Sparta hated their owners.

• Many slaves worked in the mines in ancient Greece.
• Look at this picture. List reasons why working in a mine might be difficult and uncomfortable.
• List ways that slaves helped the ancient Greeks to prosper.

WRAPPING UP

1. Were all slaves in ancient Greece mistreated? Were all treated well?
2. Review the prices of slaves in ancient Greece. Why did some slaves cost more than others?
3. Pretend you are a slave. Write a letter to your owner asking for your freedom. Consider
   (a) what you will say
   (b) your history (where you come from)
   (c) your family situation (where they are)
   (d) why your owner should set you free.
4. (a) In your own words, discuss the daily life of a slave in ancient Greece.
   (b) How did the lives of slaves differ from the lives of free people in ancient Greece? List at least three differences.
5. (a) What do you think of the ancient Greeks' attitudes towards slaves?
   (b) How would you feel if your father or mother had been taken as a slave in ancient Athens?
6. Some say that the ancient Greeks could not have created such an advanced culture and society if they did not have slaves. What do you think? If this first statement is true, was slavery worth it?

DEVELOPING YOUR SKILLS

1. Do countries today have slaves? Research slavery. Report what you find to your class. Make sure you outline the history of slavery in your country.
2. There is a lot of literature about the lives of slaves. Read a novel for young adults about slavery. Be ready to share informally with your classmates what you have found out.

MOVING ON

In this chapter you learned that ancient Greece was a slave society. Slaves were part of almost all households. They were considered property, not people. Many slaves were treated as part of the family. Others were worked to exhaustion in mines. Today slavery is not acceptable.

Now that we have gained this information, what area will you explore next? We have picked the education and language of ancient Greece. The next chapter will help you understand the importance of education and communication in a society. You will learn that ancient Greeks made some important contributions to our educational system and language.

CHAPTER

Education and Language
in Ancient Greece

DIGGING UP

1. What are some things that make a great teacher? What are some things that make a great student?
2. As you read this chapter, "dig up" some information about the philosophers of ancient Greece. Which one would you like to have had as a teacher?

WHAT WAS EDUCATION LIKE IN ANCIENT GREECE?

EDUCATION is important in any society. Education differed between city-states in ancient Greece. For example, ancient Sparta's youth received a military education to help them prepare for battles. For Sparta this was a matter of survival.

Education in ancient Athens focused more on literature, public speaking, and philosophy. These different educational systems showed the different values of the two city-states.

Ancient Greeks were educated to become contributing members of society. Many people in ancient Greece became famous for their contributions to society.

Philosophers and Scientists of Ancient Greece

Thales (636-546 BC) believed that everything in the universe was made of water. He brought ideas of geometry from Egypt to Greece. One of his important discoveries was static electricity.

Pythagoras (582-546 BC) invented many modern methods used in mathematics. His specialty was geometry. Pythagoras believed 10 was a perfect number. He understood the mathematics of music, connecting musical pitch and the length of a string on a musical instrument.

Socrates (469-399 BC) taught people to question. Leaders of Athens accused him of misleading the young and after a long trial he was condemned to death. Because he believed in accepting the will of the state, he willingly drank a cup of poison.

• *Pythagoras was an early mathematician.*
• *What is geometry?*
• *Try to think of ways Pythagoras' ideas have influenced the math you learn in school today.*

Plato (428-348 BC) was a pupil of Socrates. Plato believed that the world was made up of ideas, or forms. If you wanted to learn about a tree, for example, you discussed the "idea" of a tree. He believed the rulers of city-states should be philosophers. Plato taught at the **Academy** outside of Athens. He wrote *The Republic*, which described an ideal state.

• *Socrates was a Greek philosopher who lived in Athens.*
• *What is a philosopher?*
• *What ideas did Socrates teach?*

• *Plato was one of Socrates' most famous pupils.*
• *What was Plato's Academy?*
• *Can you think of why Plato thought rulers should be philosophers?* ➤

(sidebar continued)

Aristotle (384-322 BC) was a pupil of Plato. Aristotle was interested in philosophy, physics, zoology, and biology. Aristotle believed the world was physical. If you wanted to learn about a tree, for example, you went to the tree to study it. Aristotle believed that the Earth was the centre of the universe.

Aristotle was one of the greatest teachers of all time. Some of Aristotle's educational ideas are still used today. Many of the things you do in school are a result of his ideas. The most important of his ideas about education is that people learn from experiencing things with their senses, by seeing, smelling, and touching. He wrote many books. Among his most famous books was one called *Politics*. In this book, Aristotle wrote about how the government should be organized. Aristotle believed that government should be run by a kind **oligarchy**.

One of Aristotle's most famous students was Alexander the Great. Aristotle taught Alexander many things about Greek life and culture. Even when Alexander was in the middle of battles and conquering distant lands, he took time to send back biological specimens to Aristotle so that Aristotle could study them. After Alexander died, Aristotle fled Athens because he was disliked for his ties with Alexander and Macedonia.

• *Aristotle was one of Plato's students.*
• *What was the major difference between the teachings of Aristotle and Plato?*
• *Do you agree with Aristotle that people learn by seeing, smelling, and touching? Explain by giving examples.*

Erasistratus was a doctor. He made important discoveries about the heart and brain. As early as 290 BC, he knew that the human heart had valves. His idea that the heart was a pump helped us understand how the human body worked.

Euclid (323-285 BC) was a mathematician. He taught in Alexandria, in Egypt. He wrote about geometry and astronomy.

Aristarchus (310-230 BC) was an astronomer. He knew that the Earth moved around the sun. Although his beliefs were correct, they were abandoned for almost 2000 years. He also explained a way to measure the distance of the sun, moon, and other heavenly bodies from the Earth. His method was correct, but his instruments were poor. As a result, his distances were incorrect.

KEY FACTS

The ancient Greeks believed in educating people to become valuable contributors to their society. Many of those who contributed to Greek society have affected Western civilization as we know it today.

How Were Young People Educated in Ancient Athens?

Today, most young people attend school with boys and girls their own age. In ancient Athens, boys and girls did not attend school together. Boys and girls were treated differently.

In ancient Athens, girls did not go to school. Instead, they stayed home and learned household skills from their mothers or from slaves.

Boys started school at age six or seven. The age a boy was when he started school depended on whether his father could afford the fees. Schools in ancient Athens were private. Most boys were taught by professional tutors.

Boys in ancient Athens studied **academic** subjects. They were taught to read, write, count, play the lyre, dance, and recite poetry. Instead of learning to write on paper, boys learned to write on wax tablets. If they were working on special projects, they used **papyrus** and a split-reed pen.

In ancient Athens, the subjects boys studied were more specific than the subjects you study. There were no books like the ones we have today. The teacher in ancient Greece might read poetry from a scroll and boys memorized it by hearing and then reciting back. Or the teacher memorized the entire poem and had boys try to do the same. Most educated people in ancient Greece could recite from memory. It was a sign of culture and learning. Boys memorized Homer's *Iliad* and the *Odyssey* to recite at festivals.

Homer

Homer was a great Greek poet. As you read earlier, Homer lived in Ionia from about 750 to 700 BC. We do not know very much about him. Legend tells us that he was blind and that he wrote the *Iliad* and the *Odyssey*. His writing was so good that seven cities claim that he was born there. The teacher Aristotle admired Homer's poetry as the most beautiful writing in history. Other poets such as Virgil were inspired by it. The Greeks regard him as a genius, and his poems were memorized by Greek school children.

The *Iliad* is an **epic poem**. It tells what the Greek gods and mortals did during the last weeks of the 10-year Trojan War. After a quarrel with Agamemnon, the warrior Achilles refused to continue the battle. But Achilles' friend Patroclus was killed in a fight with Hector, the prince of Troy. Achilles became so angry that he led an attack and Hector was killed. But Achilles returned Hector's body to King Priam for a hero's funeral.

The *Odyssey* tells what happened after the *Iliad*. It too is an epic poem — 24 books in all. The story begins 10 years after the Trojan War. For seven of those years, Odysseus (also called Ulysses) was held prisoner by the nymph Calypso. Odysseus was one of the bravest and most important of all Greek warriors. The *Odyssey* tells of his amazing adventures.

Odysseus wanted badly to return home to his loving family, but Calypso always played tricks on him. His return home was delayed by visits to the land of forgetfulness and to the underworld. He fought with the one-eyed Cyclops, sea monsters, and **Sirens**.

Finally, when Odysseus returned home, he discovered that his wife Penelope was being pressured by noblemen who wanted to marry her to gain her fortune. Odysseus killed all of these noblemen and was reunited with his family.

- *Boys in ancient Athens worked and studied very hard.*
- *What school subject is being taught by this teacher?*
- *What major differences are there between your education and the education of children in ancient Athens?*

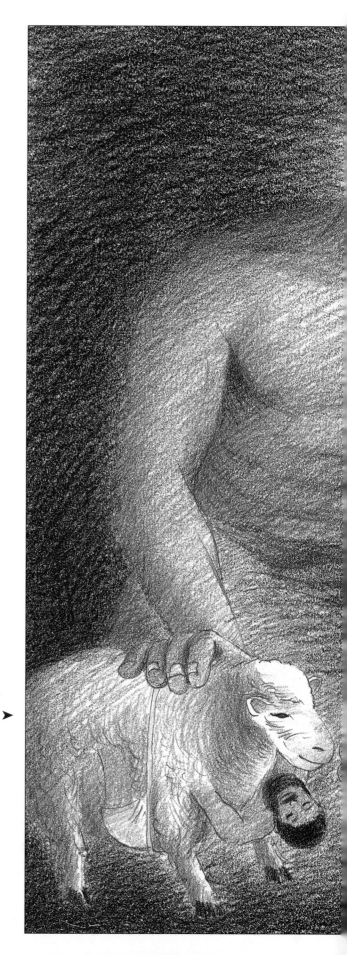

• *Homer was a Greek poet whose works are studied even today.*
• *What kind of characters appeared in his writings?*
• *Why do you think young Greek boys were taught Homer's* Iliad *and* Odyssey?

• *This picture depicts a scene from Homer's* Odyssey. *To escape* ➤
the Cyclops, Odysseus and his crew hid under the bellies of sheep.
• *The story of Odysseus and the Cyclops is a well-known Greek myth. Even if you know the story well, pretend you know only what you see in the picture. Write a short story that fits the information shown in the drawing.*
• *Who was Odysseus? Find a book of Greek myths and read about his adventures. Be ready to share what you find with others in your class.*

The ancient Athenians believed in educating both the mind and the body. In the morning, the mind was educated by studying academic subjects. In the afternoon, the boys went to the **gymnasium** to exercise their bodies.

At the gymnasium, the boys would take part in physical activities such as running, boxing, wrestling, discus hurling, javelin throwing, and long jumping with stone weights in their hands. A favourite activity for some boys was **pankration**. Pankration (meaning "all-powerful") was a combination of boxing and wrestling. Because there were few rules to keep the wrestlers from getting hurt, pankration could get very rough. During their exercises, the boys smeared their bodies with olive oil. Later they removed dirt and the oil by scraping their bodies with a tool called a **strigil**.

Many boys in ancient Greece went to school with a slave called the paedogogos. The

Western society still holds the ancient Greek idea that both the mind and the body should be trained.

paedogogos made sure that the boy practised good manners and obedience. If the boy did not, the slave used a birch switch to teach the boy an immediate lesson. Pedagogy, an English word that means teaching, comes from the name of these ancient Greek slaves.

By the age of 15, most boys in ancient Athens had finished school. If a young man wanted more education, he had to find a teacher by himself. Some students attended Plato's Academy or Aristotle's **Lyceum**. These early schools helped young people in their pursuit of knowledge. Another place to get more education was the agora, where philosophers such as Socrates taught. These classes in philosophy were some of the first **university** courses ever.

The aim of education in ancient Athens was to help the student grow both physically and mentally. Boys were trained to become citizens of their city-states. Being a citizen included being physically fit for military duty and mentally fit for leadership within the city-state. Physical education and academic education were equal in the eyes of the ancient Greeks.

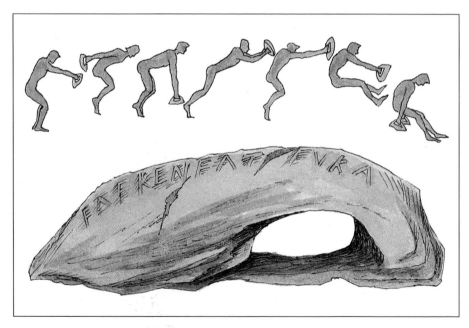

• *Athenian boys took part in physical activities such as long jumping. Long jumpers in ancient Greece did not take a running start. Instead, they swung a weight back and forth, which helped propel them farther.*

• *Using the picture, compose a set of directions that athletes might use to perform the long jump.*

• *Are physical activities important in education today?*

How Were Young People Educated in Ancient Sparta?

Education in Athens differed from education in Sparta. Education in Sparta was simple. It consisted of preparing for war. Good Spartans were good soldiers. Good soldiers were disciplined soldiers. In Sparta, discipline and obedience were key parts of the training of boys. To the Spartans, physical fitness was more important than anything else.

At the age of seven, boys were taken from their parents. They were placed in state boarding schools. At these schools, boys were taught to endure cold, hunger, and pain.

Comfort was not important to Spartans. There was no room in Sparta for weakness. In their military schools, Spartan boys learned not to be afraid of the dark, not to be picky about food, and not to cry or throw temper tantrums. They slept on beds made of hard reeds. They were allowed only one piece of clothing each year. Their hair was cut short and they went barefoot—even as they marched into battle. Stealing food was expected. It was even encouraged.

- Spartan boys trained very hard to become good fighters.
- What might the boy who is standing up say to the boy who has been knocked down?
- Why do you think the Spartans had such a strong military state?

However, not all of a Spartan's education was physical. Boys were taught to read and write. They were also taught some music. But the music had to be marching songs that the boys could sing as they marched into battle.

At age 16, each boy had to go into the country alone. In the country, the boy had to survive by using his wits. Another important task was to hunt and kill a slave. When this job was completed, the young man was considered a Spartan citizen.

Girls in Sparta were not treated like girls in Athens. Spartan girls were taught to wrestle, throw the javelin, and take part in public sports. Spartan girls needed to be strong and healthy so they could give birth to strong, healthy Spartan babies.

WHAT WAS THE GREEK LANGUAGE LIKE?

You have probably already studied the social studies concept called **interdependence**. Interdependence means that groups of people depend on each other to meet their mutual needs. Often we think that this means only trading goods and services with other people. But interdependence has a broader meaning.

The ancient Greeks were interdependent with the cultures around them. Each culture influenced the other culture. The influence of ancient Greece has not died. You have already seen many ways that ancient Greek culture has influenced us today. Another influence of the Greeks on our civilization is language. Many words we use today come from the language of ancient Greece.

For example, many English words have Greek roots or come exactly from the Greek language. Some examples are academy, democracy, drama, poet, pneumatics (air), stoic, and tyrant. Using Greek words helps us meet our need to communicate with one another better.

Where Do Words Come From?

Some words mentioned (academy, democracy, drama, poet, pneumatics, stoic, and tyrant) may be new to you. Others you may know. If you know the words already, you don't need to look them up. If these words are new to you, look them up and write a definition. The best way to learn new words is not to copy their definitions straight from the dictionary, but to write their definitions in your own words. In this way, you will learn to use them in your writing and conversation.

What Is an Alphabet?

Have you ever wondered where the word alphabet comes from? The word alphabet comes from the first two letters of the Greek alphabet, *alpha* and *beta*.

 KEY CONCEPTS Every civilization meets an important social need by educating its people. Education helps a society grow by helping it learn new things. For education to take place, every society needs a language.

The ancient Greeks were also dependent on other cultures. They borrowed good ideas wherever they could find them. The Greek alphabet was borrowed from the **Phoenicians.**

The Greek Alphabet		
	GREEK	**ENGLISH**
A	alpha	a
ß	beta	b
Γ	gamma	g
Δ	delta	d
E	epsilon	e (e as in b<u>e</u>d)
Z	zeta	z
H	eta	e (e as in <u>ea</u>t)
θ	theta	th
I	iota	i (i as in h<u>i</u>de or d<u>i</u>d)
K	kappa	k
Λ	lambda	l (l as in <u>l</u>amb)
M	mu	m
N	nu	n
Ξ	xi	x (ks as in ta<u>x</u>)
O	omicron	o (o as in g<u>o</u>t)
Π	pi	p
P	rho	r
Σ	sigma	s
T	tau	t
Y	upsilon	u, y (either oo as in b<u>oo</u>k or u as in d<u>u</u>e)
Φ	phi	ph
X	chi	k (as in <u>c</u>ool)
ψ	psi	ps (ps as in la<u>ps</u>e)
Ω	omega	o (o as in g<u>oa</u>t)

WRAPPING UP

1. How were most boys taught in ancient Greece? How were the girls taught?
2. Why did the ancient Greeks believe in educating the mind and the body?
3. Describe a day of school in ancient Greece. Compare it to your school day.
4. Make a list of your school subjects. Organize them into two lists: body, mind. Is your education more focused on the body or the mind? Why?
5. Where would you have liked to attend school, ancient Athens or ancient Sparta? Why?
6. Could the Spartan education work in your society? Why or why not?

DEVELOPING YOUR SKILLS

1. Does education serve any purpose today? Is education important in today's society? Why or why not? If you could design an educational system, what would you have in it? What subjects would you include or not include? Why?
2. Act out a scene from a school in ancient Athens. Here are some suggestions you might try: (1) a boy reciting the *Odyssey*, or (2) writing Greek words. (How about using English words that come from Greek?) The actors in your scene might include the schoolmaster, students, and the paedogogi (guardian slaves).
3. Compare your system of education to that of ancient Greece. Which system do you think is better? Why?

MOVING ON

In this chapter you learned about the way young people were educated in ancient Greece. You learned that in ancient Athens, academic subjects were important. In ancient Sparta, physical training was important.

You learned that in Athens boys went to school and girls were taught at home. The aim of education was to develop young people's minds and bodies so that they could become contributing members of their society. A similar approach is used in our society today.

In the next chapter, you will learn that ancient Greece was a growing and complex society. You will learn how the people travelled and how they traded with others for the things they needed. You will study how trading with others helps a society meet its needs.

Today, how do we meet our needs when products or services are not available? We try to find these resources somewhere else. The ancient Greeks were no different. They were willing to trade with other people. The next chapter will help you understand how the ancient Greeks used transportation and trade to meet their needs.

CHAPTER

Transportation and Trade
in Ancient Greece

DIGGING UP

1. Transportation and trade are important in every society. How has your country's landscape influenced transportation and trade?
2. As you read this chapter, "dig up" some reasons trade was important to the ancient Greeks. Do you think trade was more important to them than it is to your society today?

HOW DID PEOPLE IN ANCIENT GREECE TRAVEL?

LIKE any advanced people, the ancient Greeks travelled from place to place. There were many reasons for their travel. First, they were curious about the world around them. Second, they were anxious to trade with other people. They wanted to trade for goods they could not provide for them-

selves. These goods, like silk for clothing and wood for building, helped the people meet the important needs of their society.

Third, the ancient Greeks were often involved in wars that took them to other places. Fourth, the soil was not always fertile and would not support a large population. When the population grew too large, many ancient Greeks travelled to other places to live as **colonists**.

As the ancient Greeks travelled, they met other groups of people. These people had things the ancient Greeks wanted but did not have. As the Greeks got better at their work, they could create more products than they needed to meet their own needs. This **surplus** of products allowed them to trade with other people.

When they travelled and traded with other people, the ancient Greeks had one advantage. Their country was surrounded by water. Travelling by water is often easier than travelling by land. Greece is mountainous, and it was difficult to build good roads. Travel on land in the winter was almost impossible. Because they lived by the sea, it was natural for the ancient Greeks to move their goods and themselves by sea.

 **KEY FACTS**

The landscape of Greece determined the way the ancient Greeks transported goods. Because roads were difficult to build, the people depended on the sea for trade routes.

• *This replica of a trireme is docked at Hydra Harbour in Greece.*
• *Look at this picture and draw what you imagine the rest of the trireme would look like.*
• *Why do you think the trireme was used as a military ship?*

It did not take the people of ancient Greece long to build a strong fleet of ships. They developed different types of ships to serve different purposes.

For war, they developed powerful ships called **triremes**. Triremes were used as military ships. They were long and slender. They had three tiers of oars and one sail. On the bow of the triremes was a battering ram that was used to destroy enemy ships. The tip of the battering ram was covered with the metal bronze. It could easily slice through a wooden ship.

Merchant ships were rounder than triremes. They did not move as quickly through the water as triremes. Their purpose was to carry goods.

Travel by sea could be dangerous. In ancient Greece, sailors followed the coast. Compasses or charts had not been invented yet. Sailors could easily get lost.

Pirates were only too willing to attack a ship, steal its goods, sink it, and dump the sailors into the sea. To combat pirates, the navy of Athens became the protector of the seas. Triremes were used both in war and against pirates who dared attack the Greek merchant fleet.

 **KEY FACTS**　　Ancient Greece traded with other countries in order to provide necessary materials for their culture.

WHAT DID PEOPLE IN ANCIENT GREECE TRADE?

Ships of ancient Greece sailed all over the ancient world trading a variety of goods. Metals were important to advancing civilizations, and the ancient Greeks traded metals with other people. They exported beautiful objects of copper and bronze, olive oil, pottery, grain, and wine. Merchants brought back many things. They brought back grain and wool from Sicily, beautiful rugs from Carthage, ivory from Ethiopia, sails and papyrus from Egypt, copper from Cyprus, purple dye from Cyprus and Tyre, and metals from the Black Sea area. Merchants brought back exotic Arabian spices obtained in Asia Minor (Turkey). The ancient Greeks also **imported** slaves.

Trading with others helped the ancient Greeks meet their own needs even when the resources they needed were not available in their own country. For example, the ancient Greeks always needed more grain to make bread.

Today, how do we meet our needs when the products or services are not available? The answer is we try to find these resources elsewhere. We might find what we need in other towns, cities, or countries. When we find what we want and need, we trade our surplus for it. The ancient Greeks were no different from us. They were willing to trade goods they had for goods they wanted.

Many societies need things they do not have. Because of the climate, people might not be able to grow or manufacture what they need. Because of the geography, they might not have all the natural resources they need. What do they do? They trade with others.

Trade met a social need of ancient Greece and the societies it traded with. Trade was a way that these societies worked together to meet each other's needs.

WHAT DID THE ANCIENT GREEKS USE FOR MONEY?

All societies need a way to trade within their own society and with others. Ancient Greece was a complex society. The people needed to trade what they had for what they needed.

Early societies used a system of trade called **barter**. In this system, one person would trade with another person, item for item. It was much as you and your friends might trade hockey cards. However, a more complex society needs a more complex system of trade.

KEY CONCEPTS　　The environment affects our ability to meet our needs. Sometimes a society will trade its goods to obtain things it does not have.

 **KEY FACTS**

Ancient Greece used **currency** to simplify trade (in the place of barter). We still use currency today to trade one service for another. Each Greek city-state issued its own, unique coinage.

Why? Because not every person's work produces a product that can be bartered. For example, a banker provides a service, not a product.

The more complex the society, the more complex trade becomes. Complex societies need a method of buying and selling that allows people to trade many goods and services. In our modern, complex society that method is money.

Ancient Greek society also used a system of money. Greeks copied the idea of coins from the kingdom of Lydia, in Asia Minor, in about 650 BC. Coins were **minted** from silver, gold, bronze, and electrum (a natural alloy of gold and silver).

Special marks were **imprinted** on the coins for two reasons. First, these marks guaranteed how much metal the coin contained. Second, Greek coins were decorated on both the front and the back with pictures of gods and goddesses. These pictures were to honour the gods and goddesses.

• *Greece is a peninsula. It is surrounded by water on three sides. At ancient Greek ports, goods from all over the world were unloaded.*
• *What goods are being loaded and unloaded in this picture? Who would have used these goods?*
• *Make a list of the goods you see in this picture. For those being unloaded, where are they probably coming from? For those being loaded, where are they probably going?*

Athenian coins had an owl on one side because the owl was the bird of Athena, the patron goddess of the city. The owl is also a symbol of wisdom. During Athens' Classical Period, the Athenians tried to force other city-states to use their "owl-eyed" coins for trade. In ancient Sparta, the people used iron bars for money.

• *Ancient Athenians used an "owl-eyed" coin to exchange for goods and services.*
• *Using this picture as an example, design a coin for your city or town.*
• *Explain why the ancient Greeks moved from the barter system to the money system.*

Denominations of Currency

Money in ancient Greece had several **denominations** of currency. From smallest to largest, they were as listed here:

6 obols	=	1 drachma
4 drachmas	=	1 stater
100 drachmas	=	1 mina
60 minas	=	1 talent

Prices for Some Common Greek Goods

1 ox	=	50 - 100 drachmas
1 sheep	=	10 - 20 drachmas
1 coach	=	15 - 17 drachmas
1 table	=	4 - 6 drachmas

The money system met a social need of the ancient Greeks. This system allowed people to supply each other with the goods and services they needed. Money allowed the ancient Greeks to work together to meet their needs. The money system today serves the same purpose.

 WRAPPING UP

1. Write a definition for the following words: barter, minted, imprints.
2. Describe in your own words what it means to have "complex trade." (Hint: Think about things you trade with your friends. When does trading become difficult? Why?)
3. (a) Why do societies make currency for trade?
   (b) Pretend you are the person in charge of creating currency for trade. What important tips could you share to help people make better currency?
4. Why would it be important to imprint coins? Think of two reasons.
5. Compare the picture of an ancient Greek coin to modern coins. What similarities and differences do you see?

6. Do you think trade made life better for the ancient Greeks? Why or why not? Defend your answer.

 DEVELOPING YOUR SKILLS

1. (a) On a map, locate some of the places the ancient Greeks traded with.
   (b) Trace this map and draw on it the trading routes.
   (c) Indicate the types of items traded.
2 (a) What kinds of things do we trade?
   (b) Do you think it's right for people (for example, hockey or baseball players) to be traded? Why or why not? Present your answer to the class.

 MOVING ON

In this chapter, you learned another way the ancient Greeks met their social needs. The ancient Greeks built ships that allowed them to travel to other lands and trade with other societies. Trade was a way that ancient Greece and other societies worked together to get resources they needed.

Within ancient Greece, the people traded coins for goods and services. This money system allowed the Greeks to work together to meet their needs. As ancient Greece worked to meet its social needs, it grew and expanded as a society.

Growth and expansion make a society more complex. The more complex a society, the more organization it needs to keep running smoothly. In a society, organization usually means government. In the next chapter, you will study the government of ancient Greece.

Without some form of government, it would be almost impossible for a society to meet its social needs. All societies create ways to organize the lives of their people. If they did not, the people could not work together. The larger the society, the greater the need to work together.

As you study the next chapter, you will find out how the ancient Greeks organized to govern their own society. You will also learn that our society has borrowed many ideas from the ancient Greeks about how to govern ourselves.

C H A P T E R

Government in Ancient Greece

DIGGING UP
1. Who are the elected leaders of your community? Of your country?
2. Try to explain the purpose of government.
3. As you read this chapter, "dig up" some ways ancient Greek ideas about government have influenced how your country is governed.

HOW WAS ANCIENT GREECE GOVERNED?

LIKE most ancient governments, the government system of ancient Greece evolved slowly. The geography of Greece influenced the way city-states developed. Greece was a land of mountains and valleys. By 800 BC, it was divided into many small, separate city-states.

Before about 800 BC, kings ruled the city-states. During the early period of ancient Greece, some kings showed their wealth by building huge and elaborate palaces. Theseus, a legendary Mycenaean king, built a large palace on the Acropolis in Athens. In ancient Sparta, however, kings did not live in luxury.

They were not allowed to display any sign of wealth. They could not build large palaces, nor could they gather expensive things around them. From their youth, Spartans were taught that there was something more important than wealth and luxury — honour.

There is a wise old saying that "power corrupts," which means that a person or group of people may get too much power. When this happens, they may forget the needs of other people and think only about what they want. Ancient Greek rulers were no different from other rulers. Many worked to gain greater power and wealth. To gain greater wealth and to ensure that their city-state was protected, ancient Greek rulers married for political reasons. During the early period of the monarchy, they married women from the ruling families of other city-states.

Kingship dwindled out in the Dark Ages. Gradually, a small **clique** of wealthy families, called an **aristocracy**, replaced the kings as leaders. The aristocracy specialized in running the government of the city-states. The sons of these families ruled after their fathers' deaths. Sparta was the only exception. In Sparta, a system of government developed using two kings. The purpose of two kings was simple. One would watch the other to make sure he was acting honourably.

Boys in ancient Greece listened to poetry and stories of Greek heroes. These poems taught them that citizens should act with honour. Ancient Greeks learned these lessons well. As a result of these poems, ancient Greek leaders were very concerned with acting honourably. They had to govern by **mutual consent**. It was the only honourable way to govern.

KEY FACTS

Honour was more important to the ancient Greeks than wealth.

CASE STUDY

WHAT IS A CONSTITUTION?

Some countries are ruled by codes of laws and rules that have never been written down. England is such a country. It has an unwritten **constitution**. Many other countries have written constitutions. These constitutions describe the rules and **principles** by which the people are governed. Canada and the United States have written constitutions. All laws in both countries are developed from principles written into their constitutions.

Why would a country want a written constitution? One reason is so people will be able to understand what, exactly, the rules are. People from all societies believe that when something is written, it becomes more powerful. Another reason people want a constitution is that they believe it will stop one person or group from getting too much power. They believe too much power corrupts.

1. What is a constitution?
2. Can you name other groups or organizations that may have constitutions?
3. Do you think it is important to have a constitution? Why or why not?
4. Make up a constitution for your classroom or school.

The power of the aristocracy declined because people resented the **favours** that the rich were given. Between 600 BC and 500 BC, some important city-states of ancient Greece were ruled by **tyrants** who took power using new soldiers called **hoplites**. A tyrant was like a king in that he could rule any way he wanted to. The difference between a king and a tyrant was the king ruled by birth, but the tyrant ruled by taking power through force. Many tyrants were very good to their people. For example, Peisistratus was a good tyrant to the people of Athens.

During the Classical Period of ancient Greece, the people began to develop two important customs. First, they believed that the leadership of the city-state should be passed around, by election, from one leading family to another. Second, leaders were to follow specific rules about how the city-state should be run. Every Greek city-state developed the custom of elections and of following a set of rules — an unwritten constitution. Our own idea of **constitutional law** developed from these customs.

Social Status Within Ancient Greek City-States

The term status means standing, rank, importance, or position within a group. In ancient Greece, not everyone was equal. Some people held a more important rank, or status, within the city-state. Statesmen had the highest status. The second most important people were the military leaders, followed by soldiers, citizens, women, children, and slaves.

HOW WAS ANCIENT ATHENS GOVERNED?

In Athens, in 508-507 BC, a new form of government called democracy was begun. In this form of government, all male citizens of the city-state met in a gathering called the Assembly to vote on matters of importance to the city-state. Jurymen, officials, and council members were elected to positions in the government.

If a citizen were elected to a post in the government, he would keep his other jobs. Government in ancient Greece was a part-time job. Still, helping to run the city-state was considered one of the most important tasks a Greek citizen could perform.

• This hoplite was one of the soldiers who helped tyrants take power between 600 and 500 BC in ancient Greece.
  • What can you tell about hoplites from this picture?
  • How were tyrants similar to and different from kings and aristocrats in ancient Greece?

KEY FACTS

The ancient Greeks developed a form of government called democracy. Democracy means "rule by the people." Democracy became the model for modern government in the Western world. In ancient Greece, democracy was limited to Greek men. Women, children, immigrants, and slaves were not allowed to vote.

The Government Structure of Ancient Athens

Boule

The boule was the council of 500 citizens. It was split into 10 groups of 50 citizens. Each group took turns leading the boule for one-tenth of the year (a little more than 36 days). The 50 presidents of the boule lived and ate in the tholos (round hall). The entire council of 500 met every day except for festival days in the bouleterion (council house) in the Agora. The citizens of the boule had two main jobs. First, they prepared items for the Assembly. Second, they supervised public officials.

The Council of Areopagus

The Council of Areopagus was made up of former judges. These judges were called **archons**. The council's job was to run the religious festivals. They also tried cases of treason, arson, and murder.

The Ecclesia (The Assembly)

Assembly is a word that means the gathering together of a group. The Athenian Assembly was called the Ecclesia. It was the gathering together of Athenian citizens. All citizens could attend. The meeting was run by the 50 presidents of the boule. It met once a month at dawn on the Pnyx, near the Acropolis. After a religious ceremony, the Assembly heard proposals from the council. The proposals were discussed and then voted on. Taxes, declarations of war, or spending of money could not happen unless the Assembly approved.

Government Officials

GENERALS: Ten generals were elected each year. These generals were military and political leaders. Citizens could run for consecutive terms.

TREASURY OFFICIALS: Treasury officials collected fines, taxes, made contracts, and leased property. They controlled all public funds. These funds were stored in the Parthenon.

MINOR OFFICIALS: Minor officials were in charge of the police force. They also collected minor taxes, supervised the storage of weapons, provided animals for sacrificing, and ran athletic contests.

LAW COURTS: In law courts in ancient Greece, cases were tried by jury. The crowds at law courts were very large. They had to be. Every year, 6000 jurymen were chosen by a draw. The size of the jury depended on the case.

The jury voted by placing one of two tokens into an urn. If they put in the token with a hole in it, it meant that they believed the person on trial was guilty. If they put in the token without a hole, it meant they believed that the person on trial was not guilty. The archon counted the votes and announced the result.

• In Athens, jurymen used tokens to vote on the guilt or innocence of a person on trial.
• Why do you think the tokens were small enough to fit into a person's hand?
• Find out more on jury trials in Athens, for example: How were these tokens used at a trial? How large was the jury? Who could be on it?

There were two systems of appointment in Athenian democracy: election and lot. High-ranking officials such as generals, archons (judges), and treasurers were chosen by elections in the Assembly. Lesser officials and council members (the boule) were selected by lot. When your name was drawn by lot, it was your turn.

The Roles of Citizens in Ancient Athens

Within government in Athens, there were three main roles:

1. Council members (the boule) controlled public officials and set up the agenda for discussion at the Assembly.

2. Jurymen heard and judged arguments between citizens. There were no lawyers. You could ask an **orator** to state your case if you didn't have the skills yourself.

3. Archons were elected to run festivals and administer laws.

The protection and security of the Greek city-state was the most important job of the government. Because security was so crucial, some Greek laws were harsh. In Athens, a citizen could write on a piece of broken pottery called an "ostracon" the name of a dangerous person. If a number of ostraca were handed to the Assembly with the dangerous person's name on them, he or she was banished from the city for 10 years. From this practice comes the word **ostracism**.

HOW WAS ANCIENT SPARTA GOVERNED?

The government of Sparta differed from the governments of other city-states. Sparta had two kings. These kings had two main jobs. One was to keep an eye on each other. The second and most important job of the Spartan kings was to train the Spartan army for war.

Aside from the kings, there were five officials, called "ephors," who were elected every year. There was a council of 28 elders and an Assembly of all adult male Spartans.

Every free man of Sparta who was physically able was trained to be a soldier. At the age of 60, a man could be chosen as a council member. His job was to help govern the city-state.

There were three classes of people in Sparta. The first class were the Spartans. The Spartans were the ruling class. They ruled by force. The second class were the free men. The free men included artisans and farmers called **perioeci**. The perioeci had no political rights. The third class were the Helots. The Helots were Greek serfs who outnumbered the true-blooded Spartans. The Helots were the slaves of Sparta.

Spartans feared that the Helots would overthrow their rule. To stop secret meetings among Helots, Spartans made a law that Helots were not allowed out at night. To enforce this law, Spartans roamed the streets at night. If they found a Helot out of doors, the Helot would be killed immediately.

A Who's Who of Government in Ancient Greece

Solon lived about 600 BC. He was an early leader of Athens. He reorganized citizens into four classes based on wealth. Wealth was based on how much a farm produced. By working hard, people could move into a higher class. For example, if their farm produced more, they could move from being a second-class citizen to being a first-class citizen. Solon also reformed Athens' harsh laws.

Cleisthenes lived about 510 BC. He changed Solon's system of classes. His system was based on 10 classes composed of a cross-section of Athenian society. Its purpose was to decrease the power of rich families and create more equality among classes. Cleisthenes introduced the practice of banning people suspected of interfering with the government.

Pericles (495-429 BC) raised Athens to its glory by beautifying it with temples and sculptures. One such temple was the Parthenon. Pericles established a common currency for use among the city-states. Pericles perfected the democracy of Athens. The freedom of the individual was very important to Pericles.

Themistocles was the leader of Athens during the Persian Wars. He was archon in 493 BC. He worked to make Athens' navy stronger and make the port leading to Athens more difficult to attack. His idea of making Athens' navy strong eventually made Athens a powerful city-state. He was ostracized in 472 BC for being too proud and for engaging in secret dealings with Persia. He ended his days a governor of a Greek city subject to Persia.

Lycurgas lived about 675 BC. He may have been responsible for reforming the Spartan constitution and for introducing the Spartan military way of life.

• This man was a member of the perioeci.
• What foods are in this picture? From your knowledge of Greek geography, why would fish be an important part of the diet of the people?
• What rights did the perioeci have in Spartan society?

WRAPPING UP

1. Using the glossary, define democracy, aristocrat, ostracism.
2. What was the purpose of the Assembly? Who does this work today in your country?
3. How is your country's government similar to the government of ancient Athens? How is it different?
4. Contrast the differences between the government of ancient Athens and ancient Sparta.
5. (a) In your opinion, which style of government would serve your needs best? Why?
   (b) Make an election poster that would tell other people the reasons they should vote for your choice.
6. (a) Do you think that the practice of ostracism was fair? Why or why not?
   (b) What problems might you run into if we used this practice today?

DEVELOPING YOUR SKILLS

1. (a) Pretend you have a chance to interview a person who has been ostracized for some behaviour. Write down his or her response to whether ostracism is fair or not.
   (b) (Art) Using pieces of broken plant pots, make an ostracon. (Write an ancient Greek name on it using the Greek alphabet.)
2. (Drama) From your class, elect some judges, council members, and public officials. Hold an assembly meeting to discuss an issue that would be important to the Athenians. For example, should we go to war with Sparta? Or have citizens defend themselves in a mock trial over a typical issue such as grazing land.

3. Think about the reasons life developed in ancient Greece the way it did. Set up a series of cause-and-effect relationships that suggest how one activity affected another. (For example, how did the ancient Greek belief in a healthy body affect their lifespan?)

MOVING ON

In this chapter, you learned that many Western governments have borrowed the idea of democracy from ancient Greece. You learned that democracy was a slow process that took shape over a long period of time.

As you studied the ancient Greek system of government, you learned about the strengths and weaknesses of their city-states. Is it possible that some future generation might study our society's way of governing to make a better, fairer way to govern its society?

In the next chapter, you will learn that the people in ancient Greece were like every other society. They had problems. Things did not always go smoothly. The people faced struggles, including wars.

All societies face problems. The strength of a society can be tested by how it survives the hard times it faces. Ancient Greece was a wealthy society. Other societies wanted to take away what the ancient Greeks had. The result was that ancient Greeks fought many wars.

One way to learn more about ancient Greece is to study how the people faced threats to their society. Like people in all societies, the ancient Greeks needed to defend themselves. If they did not, their society would not survive. In the next chapter, you will learn about some of the wars the ancient Greeks fought.

CHAPTER

12

Defence and War in Ancient Greece

DIGGING UP

1. Many countries today have an army, even though they are not involved in war. Why do you think a country would have an army during peacetime?

2. As you read this chapter, "dig up" some reasons the navy was important to ancient Athens. Who joined the army in ancient Greece?

WHAT WERE THE PERSIAN WARS?

THE Persians and the ancient Greeks were enemies. For more than 50 years, during the first half of the 5th century BC, the Persians brought their huge armies against the Greeks. Although the Persians had more soldiers, the Greeks usually won the battles.

Eventually, the Greeks forced the Persians into an agreement favourable to Greece. The Persian Wars forced ancient Greeks to cooperate to fight a common enemy. This cooperation increased Greek **nationalism** and for a short time encouraged the city-states to stop fighting among themselves.

The major battles of the Persian Wars included the Battle of Marathon, the Battle of Thermopylae, and the Battle of Salamis.

The Battle of Marathon

The Greek cities on the eastern coast of the Mediterranean had been ruled by the great Persian Empire. These cities did not like Persian rule. Athens helped these cities revolt. But the Persian Empire was strong, and even the aid of Athens could not keep these cities from being defeated.

Darius, the King of Persia, was angry with Athens. He wanted to punish its people for encouraging the revolt. He massed a huge army and sailed toward the Greek plain of Marathon. There, at the bay of Marathon, he and his army of about 30,000 Persians landed.

The Athenian army numbered about 11,000. When the Athenians saw that they were outnumbered, they sent Pheidippides, their messenger, to Sparta to ask for help. But the Spartans were involved in a religious festival. They refused to send aid until the festival was over.

Miltiades, the Athenian leader, could wait no longer. Quickly, he attacked. His lightning attack surprised the Persians. In their confusion, they fled to their ships. When he saw that the Persians had retreated, Pheidippides ran to Athens to spread the good

• *Persian soldiers used weapons and armour that were different from Greek soldiers.*

• *Compare this Persian soldier to the Greek hoplite on page 85. How does the equipment of the two soldiers differ?*

• *What needs did soldiers provide for the ancient societies of Persia and Greece? What needs did a soldier have when he was away from home? How might these needs have been met?*

news. There, at the end of his 26 mile, 385 yard run (42.2 kilometres), he delivered his message and then collapsed and died. His heroic run gave the **marathon** race its name. The death toll of the Battle of Marathon was 192 Greeks and 6400 Persians.

Fearing that the Persians would sail to Athens and attack there, Miltiades rushed his hoplites back to Athens. But the Persians decided to return home rather than face another fierce battle with Athens.

The Battle of Thermopylae

The Battle of Marathon was a great victory for the Athenians. To the Persians, it was a bitter defeat. When King Darius died, his son Xerxes decided to avenge his father's defeat at Marathon. He gathered a huge army of 300,000 men to invade Greece. The Greeks would stand no chance against such a large army, Xerxes thought.

The Greeks knew they were outnumbered, but they had a plan. Rather than meet the

Major Battles of the Persian Wars

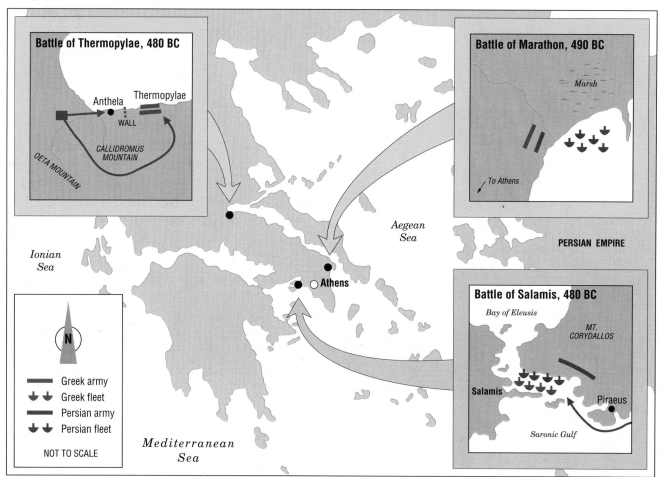

- This map shows the sites of three major battles in the Persian Wars.
- By looking at this map, can you tell which battle happened at a mountain pass?
- How were the Greeks saved by "wooden walls"? (Read on in the text to find out.)

huge Persian army in the open, they waited for the Persians at a narrow mountain pass called Thermopylae. When the Persians tried to come through the pass, the Greeks attacked them.

For three days, King Leonidas of Sparta, with 300 Spartans and a few thousand other Greeks, held off thousands of Persians. The Persians might not have won this battle, but a Greek traitor showed them a path that led through the mountains to a place behind the Greek lines. The Persians attacked the Greek defence from behind.

When King Leonidas saw that the battle was hopeless, he ordered the other Greeks to safety. He and his 300 Spartans stayed to defend the pass. Every Spartan soldier was killed. Years later, a memorial was placed at the site of this great battle. It read, "Go tell the Spartans, stranger passing by, / that here obedient to their will we lie."

• After the Battle of Thermopylae in 480 BC, the Greeks defeated the Persian navy at the Battle of Salamis. This picture shows what happened at Salamis.
• What battle plan is being used in this picture?
• After reading the information on the next page, describe how the Greeks won the Battle of Salamis.

The Battle of Salamis

The Battle of Thermopylae did not end the Persian Wars. The **oracle** of Delphi told the Greeks that they would be saved by "wooden walls." Themistocles, a general of Athens, persuaded the Athenians to build warships. These warships were to be the wooden walls that would save Athens.

The Greeks lured the Persian fleet into the Salamis channel. Here, the Greek triremes rammed the larger Persian boats. Before they were finished, they had destroyed the Persian navy. While his navy was being destroyed, Xerxes watched from a nearby hill.

The following year, the remainder of the Persian army was defeated at Plataea. Most of the important Greek city-states, led by Sparta, joined to defeat the mighty Persian army for good.

Important Dates of the Persian Wars

490 BC: King Darius of Persia sends an army to Greece. His army is defeated by the Greeks on the plain of Marathon.

480 BC: Greeks defend the Pass at Thermopylae against thousands of Persians. Three hundred Spartans fight to their deaths. The Persians finally break through. They reach Athens and capture it, burning the temples in the Acropolis.

480 BC: At the Battle of Salamis, the Greek navy destroys the Persian navy. Xerxes, the Persian king, returns home, leaving his army in Greece under the command of his son-in-law.

479 BC: The Persian army in central Greece is defeated at Plataea, northwest of Athens. Persia never invades Greece again.

 **KEY CONCEPTS**

Civilizations have met threats to their way of living by training some of their people to defend the land from invading forces.

Important People of the Persian Wars

PERSIA'S LEADERS

Darius was the king of Persia who attacked mainland Greece in 490 BC. His army was defeated on the plain of Marathon.

Xerxes was the son of Darius. He invaded Greece in 480 BC. Although many men in his army were killed, Xerxes had some success and captured Athens. However, as he watched from a hillside, his navy was badly defeated at Salamis.

ATHENS' LEADERS

Miltiades was an Athenian general. He defeated the Persians at Marathon. Later he was defeated at Paros (an island that had sided with Persia). He never got over this defeat and died in disgrace.

Themistocles was an Athenian general. He defeated the Persians at Salamis and rebuilt the walls of Athens as a way to discourage more Persian attacks. He was later ostracized for taking bribes.

SPARTA'S LEADERS

Leonidas was a king of Sparta. With 300 Spartan soldiers, he held off thousands of Persians at the pass of Thermopylae. Every Spartan, including King Leonidas, was killed.

Pausanias was the Spartan leader who defeated the Persians at Plataea. Later, Pausanias was accused of plotting with the Persians against his own people. He was starved to death as punishment.

• *Leonidas was a king of Sparta.*
• *How can you tell that Leonidas was not a cavalryman?*
• *Are there any statues in your city or town? Who are they of? Why were the statues erected?*

so strong that other city-states joined with Athens in an alliance called the **Delian League**. Members of the Delian League paid Athens to protect them against pirates or enemy attacks by another city-state.

A favourite Athenian naval tactic was to sweep close to the enemy boat. As they passed the enemy boat, their oarsmen would pull in their oars. The Athenian ship's battering ram would shear off the other ship's oars. Without oars, the enemy ship could only float in the water, helpless.

Athenian Ships

Athenian triremes had three tiers of oars, two steering paddles at the stern, one on either side, and a sail. Triremes were small compared to cargo vessels. Triremes were about 40 metres long and 5 metres across. They carried about 200 people.

WHY WAS THE ATHENIAN NAVY STRONG?

The Greeks won the Persian Wars because they had built a strong navy. The backbone of this navy was a warship called a trireme. Triremes had a simple but effective job. They would ram enemy ships with a battering ram until the ships sank.

It made sense for the ancient Greeks to build a navy. They were traders who lived on a peninsula surrounded by water. Without a strong navy, they would be at the mercy of pirates and thieves. The Athenian navy was

WHAT WAS THE ARMY IN ANCIENT GREECE LIKE?

The army in ancient Greece was one of the best of its day. Foot soldiers were known as hoplites. Every citizen of Athens was required to do two years of military service, sometime between the ages of 18 and 60.

To find out if you were chosen to serve in the military, you would go to the agora and read the list that hung there. There you would find who was selected for service that year.

In Greek city-states, being a citizen and being a soldier were almost the same thing.

The citizen's job was to protect and, if needed, die for the city-state. Today's soldiers get their equipment from the military. In ancient Greece, each soldier provided his own equipment. If you were a soldier, the armour you had depended on what you could afford to buy. The richer the soldier, the better his equipment.

Only the very rich had horses. Sometimes, fighting from a horse was a great advantage. But horses were not as important to the Greeks as they were to other armies. On the rough Greek countryside, the cavalry was not very efficient. Stirrups had not been invented yet, and it was easy to fall or be pushed off the horse. The hoplite was the best soldier for the Greek terrain.

Hoplite soldiers carried a shield, a double-edged sword, and usually a spear. A hoplite's shield carried the city-state's emblem. For example, the troops from Sparta carried the crest of that city-state.

Greek soldiers were very disciplined. In battle, they marched side by side. As they marched, each soldier protected the man on his left with his shield. This battle formation was called a **phalanx**.

Before the Persian Wars, there were many wars between Greek city-states. These wars had many causes. For example, one city-state might have a lack of crops or animals, and would attack another city-state to gain these things. Some wars lasted only a day, others for

• The Greeks used a military formation called the "phalanx." It was a very strong defensive formation during combat.
• Using the information in the picture, describe the phalanx position.
• Why was the phalanx such a strong formation?

Ancient Greeks lived with the threat of war. Being a citizen and being a soldier were almost the same thing.

only a week. Most Greek wars were fought in the summer.

In ancient Greece, there were many ways to fight a war. Sometimes armies wouldn't fight each other at all. Instead of attacking the opposition army, one army would march into another city-state and destroy the other city-state's crops—especially the olive trees. To destroy the enemy's olive trees was considered a great victory but not an honourable thing to do. The invading army might destroy grain and other crops as well.

Often one army would lay **siege** to an opposing city-state. The army would surround the city-state and try to starve the people out. At other times, bloody battles were fought hand-to-hand. To protect themselves from invaders, most city-states built a stone wall around the central core. A wall was also built around a hill called an acropolis. From this high point, people could roll rocks down on attackers trying to scale the walls.

HOW DID THE PELOPONNESIAN WAR HARM ANCIENT GREECE?

After Greece had won great victories in the Persian Wars, the Athenians were paid by other city-states to continue the fight against Persia. Instead of remaining part of the Delian League, Athens took the money it was paid and spent some of it on new buildings and temples. The Parthenon, for example, was built with this money.

The Delian League held great promise that the city-states of ancient Greece would learn to work together and develop a sense of nationalism. But, to the other city-states, Athens seemed to be turning the Delian League

 **KEY FACTS**   City-states fought among themselves. Their fighting weakened Greece, making it easy to conquer.

into the Athenian Empire. This empire was financed with the money that Athens' allies paid to be protected from Persia.

The Spartans had chosen not to join the Delian League when it was formed. Now Sparta was worried about Athens' growing presence in Greek affairs. After 460 BC, Athens started a series of wars between the two city-states that lasted about 60 years. This war was called the Peloponnesian War.

Sparta proved to be a tough opponent. Finally, Athens surrendered to Sparta in 404 BC. For a time, the democracy of Athens was replaced by Spartan rule. Spartan rule was harsh. Other Greeks found Spartan rule difficult, and they revolted. Eventually the city-state of Thebes defeated Sparta in 371 BC.

The city-states of ancient Greece were weak after years of war. Northeast of Greece was a kingdom called Macedonia. Philip, the ruler of Macedonia, saw that Greece was weak. Athens tried to stop Philip from expanding his kingdom in the north and increasing his power in the Black Sea area. Philip attacked Greece and defeated it. Philip was murdered in 336 BC. His son, Alexander the Great, became the ruler of Macedonia and Greece. The civilization of ancient Greece was ending.

- During the Peloponnesian War, the city-states of Athens and Sparta fought against each other.
- From the picture, what can you tell about the impact of the war on Greek women and children?
- What were the causes of the Peloponnesian War? What was the result?

WRAPPING UP

1. Who fought in the Peloponnesian War? What was the main reason for the fighting?
2. Summarize some events that led to the Peloponnesian War.
3. (a) Why was the Delian League so important to Greek city-states?
   (b) What other alliances do you know about that have been similar to the Delian League?
4. Contrast the differences between the armies of ancient Greece and armies today. You may need to look at other resource books.
5. Why do you think countries join in alliances? Are alliances always good? When might they cause problems? (Hint: What problems did the Delian League create among city-states in ancient Greece?)
6. The Greeks were constantly fighting among themselves. This constant fighting made them easy to conquer. Why? What does this say about nations going to war?

DEVELOPING YOUR SKILLS

1. Write a letter to Sparta or Athens. Warn them about the danger of constantly fighting each other. Try to help them understand the importance of negotiating and accepting the differences of other people. Write a reply from Sparta or Athens, keeping in mind their point of view. Will their reply end the war or will they keep on fighting? (You decide.)
2. Write a newspaper report of one battle discussed in this chapter. Try to write two reports, one from each side.

MOVING ON

In this chapter, you learned about some wars the ancient Greeks fought. You also learned that, when a society fights wars, it grows weaker. In a war, even the winner loses. The wars weakened the society of ancient Greece. The people were eventually conquered by others.

You have learned how the ancient Greeks met their physical and social needs. Now you will learn how the ancient Greeks worked to meet their psychological needs.

Psychological needs are important to study. Psychological needs are very personal. Each day you spend much of your time meeting your psychological needs. They include what we read, what we believe about life and death, what we like to do in our spare time, the type of sports we play, and other activities we like doing. The ancient Greeks met their psychological needs in many ways.

In the next chapter, you will study some activities the ancient Greeks enjoyed as a society — things like **festivals**. As you read, think about how you entertain yourself.

PART IV

Meeting Psychological Needs

Humans are like other life forms in many ways. Like plants and other animals, humans must have their physical needs satisfied, or they will not be able to survive from one day to the next. Without food, water, clothing, and shelter, a human would not be able to survive for long. But humans have many needs that plants and animals do not have.

All humans must satisfy social needs. They must organize into families and into governments. If humans are to get stronger, they must also organize themselves into many different groups.

Humans also need to meet psychological needs. They cannot always work. They must rest as well. It is a very human trait to give meaning to certain things or activities. For example, humans must eat. Who they eat with and how they eat is also important.

Humans must exercise or they will become weak. When the ancient Greeks created the Olympic games, they were doing more than exercising. When they talked about philosophy at the agora, they were doing something very special for their culture. They were meeting their psychological needs.

The next section of this book will tell you some ways in which the ancient Greeks met their psychological needs.

Entertainment in Ancient Greece

DIGGING UP

1. Can you think of some festivals you participate in every year? Have you ever been to a special festival that happens only once in a while?

2. Festivals were an important part of life in ancient Greece. As you read this chapter, "dig up" some ways festivals entertained ancient Greeks. Compare ancient Greek festivals to the ones you participate in.

HOW DID ENTERTAINMENT HELP MEET THE NEEDS OF ANCIENT GREEKS?

YOU'VE already read quite a bit about ancient Greece and the people who lived there. Do you think ancient Greece would be an enjoyable place to grow up in? Imagine that you were suddenly transported in time back to ancient Greece to live.

What would you like about living there? What would you miss most about your world?

If you are like most of us, you probably would miss the things you enjoy doing. Would you miss the modern conveniences? School? Entertainment? If you said that you might miss your entertainment, your answer shows that you already understand some differences between ancient Greece and your world.

Young people in ancient Greece did not entertain themselves in the same way you do.

KEY CONCEPTS

Entertainment meets social and psychological needs. Entertainment gives people a chance to relax from everyday tasks. It also is a time to meet people.

There were no television sets or computer games, for example. That doesn't mean there was nothing to do. Like all people, ancient Greeks created entertainment to meet their own needs. You might not enjoy the same things that young people in ancient Greece enjoyed, but they did have a variety of ways to entertain themselves.

WHAT WERE FESTIVALS LIKE IN ANCIENT GREECE?

If you like festivals, you might have enjoyed living in ancient Greece. Festivals differed, depending on the city-state. Each city-state had its own **patron** deity. Festivals were held throughout the year to honour the patron **deity** and a variety of other gods.

- *When the ancient Greeks attended festivals, they always brought gifts for the god or goddess they were honouring.*
- *What offerings are being brought to the Acropolis? List as many as you can see.*
- *Review the text. What festival are the people in the drawing attending? Who does this festival honour?*

Depending on the needs of the gods, each festival was different. Over the years, traditions grew. Each festival developed certain **rites** that people followed. Most of these rites were followed by a sacrifice (usually a cow), eating, and drinking.

One of the most important festivals in ancient Greece was Panathenaea in Athens. This festival was held in honour of Athena, the goddess of wisdom. It was held at the dawning of the first moon in the new year, in Hekatombaion (July).

During the Festival of Panathenaea, a procession of people and animals marched to the statue of Athena in the Acropolis. The centre of attention was the new sacred robe a group of young women carried for the statue. The long procession consisted of priests, officials, cavalry, charioteers, musicians, and citizens of Athens. Each person who marched carried a gift for the goddess. Most often, these gifts were objects important to the people's lives, such as vases, cups, shields, or spears.

When the marchers reached the statue of Athena, the animals were sacrificed. The new robe was placed on the statue. Then, for two days, the people celebrated. These celebrations included games, singing, dancing, and poetry competitions.

Athens had at least seven festivals a year. There were at least three festivals of Dionysus a year. The important drama festival, the Greater Dionysia, was held in March. This festival celebrated Dionysus, the god of wine, song, and fertility. During this festival, a competition among playwrights was held at the Theatre of Dionysus.

Today, we celebrate special days. Festivals and celebrations are important because they help us to remember the important events in our lives.

The dramas that were part of these festivals continue to survive as plays. These ancient Greek festivals gave us the dramatic ideas of **tragedy** and **comedy**. In a way, whenever you go to a movie, attend a live theatre performance, or put on your own plays, you are following the heritage of the ancient Greeks.

WHAT DID ANCIENT GREEKS DO FOR EVERY-DAY ENTERTAINMENT?

Ancient Greece stressed athletic and military contests because being physically fit helped protect the city-state. A fine body was a source of pride. Ancient Greeks expressed their pride and strength by exercising naked. The word gymnasium comes from the Greek language. It means "the place where men go naked." The gymnasium was a place where citizens spent their leisure time. They exercised, bathed, and discussed philosophy and political ideas.

The Olympic games and festivals were special events in ancient Greece. They did not happen every day. For everyday entertainment, the ancient Greeks played games and enjoyed

• *Children in ancient Greece played with toys, much like children in our society do.*
• *This picture is based on artifacts found in ancient Greek homes. What are the differences between the toys in this picture and the toys children play with today? What are the similarities?*
• *Write a short story about what is happening in this picture. What has happened to make the child cry?*

long conversations. In this way, they were much like we are today.

Most of the games played by ancient Greeks were physical games. One non-athletic game they did play was with dice. They also played a few games using a board and moving pieces around it. **Draughts** were played as well.

Archaeologists and historians have studied pictures and artifacts from the ancient Greek civilization. They believe that children had many toys. They played with dolls, toy animals, doll houses, and toy dishes. Children in ancient Athens played with hoops and balls. They also played a game much like field hockey. Many children had pets. Dogs were popular pets, as they are today.

🔑 **KEY FACTS**

Entertainment gave the ancient Greeks a way to build and share common interests and beliefs. It helped them unite as one people. Playing games is a good example of how this worked.

WRAPPING UP

1. Name three places that people in ancient Greece went to be entertained.
2. In your own words, describe what it would be like to go to a festival in ancient Greece.
3. (a) Describe what you do for entertainment on a typical day. On a special day?
   (b) Write a description of three things ancient Greek people did for entertainment. Then, write a description of three things you do for entertainment. How are these things similar? How are they different?
4. What games did ancient Greek children play? Think about these games. If children from ancient Greece could come to visit you, what games would they find most like the games they played in Greece?
5. Take a look at the picture of children's toys from ancient Greece. How are they similar to some toys children play with today? How are they different?
6. Why do you think people need entertainment? What important needs does it serve? Explain your answer.

DEVELOPING YOUR SKILLS

1. Design an ancient Greek game that could be played by children in your country. Write down the rules and things you will need to make to play the game.
2. List five of your favourite toys or games from either the present or from when you were younger. Compare the games you enjoyed with ancient Greek children's games and toys. Look beyond the toy to the activity taking place. Even though the toys are different, are there any similarities among the activities? If so, what?
3. Take some time to watch young children at play. What do you think? Have children really changed in 2000 years? Why or why not?

MOVING ON

In this chapter, you learned about how the ancient Greeks entertained themselves. You learned about the festivals they celebrated. You also learned why they celebrated them. You learned that these festivals were quite different from those of today. You may have seen some similarities, too.

Today, we continue to celebrate many festivals. Festivals help us relax. They allow us to share laughter and good times with people we care about. When we get together to celebrate, relax, and enjoy the company of our friends, we are working to meet our psychological needs.

The ancient Greeks worked to meet their psychological needs much as we work to meet our own. In the next chapter, you will study another similarity between today's culture and the culture of the ancient Greeks. The ancient Greeks loved the theatre. So do we.

In the next chapter, you will learn that today's theatre has been influenced by the ancient Greeks. As you read, think about some ways our theatre is similar to the theatre the ancient Greeks enjoyed.

CHAPTER

Theatre in Ancient Greece

DIGGING UP

1. Have you ever seen a play? If so, describe what you enjoyed most about the play. If you have not been to a play, write about what you would expect to see at one.
2. As you read this chapter, "dig up" ways that ancient Greek theatre has influenced entertainment in your country today.

HOW DID THEATRE HELP MEET THE NEEDS OF ANCIENT GREEKS?

AMONG the greatest gifts people of ancient Greece have given to us are their arts and literature. Many of us enjoy ideas from the ancient Greek theatre every time we watch a favourite television program or movie, or read a favourite book.

The theatre began as a way to honour the gods and goddesses. Going to the theatre was an important part of the religious life of ancient Greeks.

People enjoyed the theatre as much as we do. The famous theatre at Epidauras had more than 14,000 seats. This theatre was built so well that it had perfect acoustics. A person sitting in the seat farthest from the stage could hear the actors whisper.

Theatres were outside, in the open air. Tiers of seats were built around an open, circular space called the **orchestra**. A chorus of singers or **chanters** danced and sang on the dirt floor of the orchestra pit. The actors acted on a low stage. As is true today, the dressing rooms were backstage.

Originally, theatre in ancient Greece was only a chorus that sang songs and told stories of the gods. In later times, a man stepped out of the chorus line to speak a part. Then a second actor was added, and later still, a third. All the parts, even the women characters, were acted by men. Each actor played several roles—sometimes five.

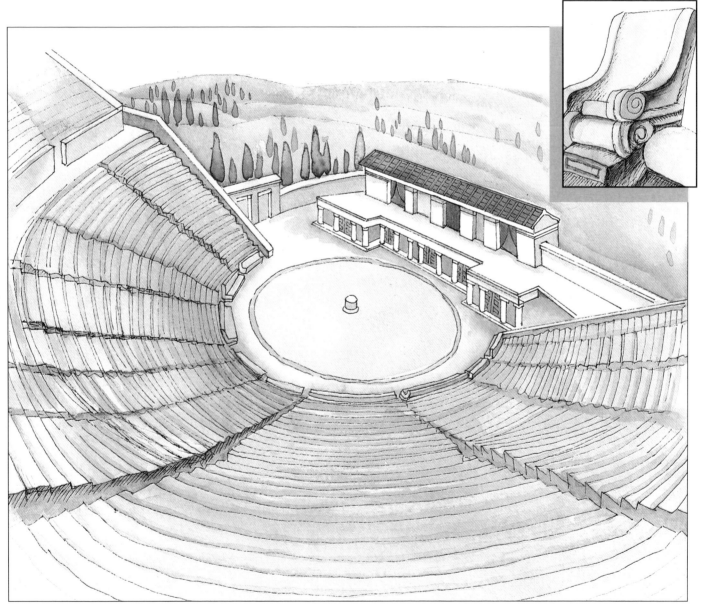

• The ancient Greeks attended plays in open-air theatres built into the sides of hills. Judges, priests, and honoured guests sat in special chairs.
• What is the shape of the Greek theatre? Why was it shaped this way?
• What modern structures are built using this design?

 **KEY FACTS**

Theatre in ancient Greece was very popular. The ancient Greeks built huge open-air theatres in which sound carried well. People who watched the play could hear it clearly no matter how far away from the stage they sat.

Actors wore exaggerated masks and platform shoes so that the audience could see them. The masks also helped magnify the actors' voices.

In ancient Greece, it didn't cost much to attend the theatre. Both rich and poor could attend. The price for a theatre ticket was two obols, a third of a drachma. If you couldn't afford the price of a ticket, you could still go to the theatre. The city-state paid your admission.

• An actor in a Greek tragedy would have worn a mask like this one in the later Hellenistic Period.
• What parts of this mask make the character look tragic?
• How are masks used in entertainment today?

• This mask was used in some ancient Greek comedies.
• What sort of character do you think this mask shows?
• What devices or methods do actors today use to play a character?

CASE STUDY

A DIFFERENT SENSE OF TIME

Today, time is very important. Many of you probably wear a watch, which you constantly look at—especially in school. Some of you even keep schedules and appointment books. You see half-hour shows on television and listen to three-minute songs on the radio. When things last longer than a half-hour, they might seem to drag on. You might become anxious to do something else.

How different time is for you than it was for the ancient Greeks. They never looked at their watches, because they didn't have them. There were no alarm clocks. (How do you suspect an alarm clock got its name?) An ancient Greek got up when the sun rose and went to bed when the sun set.

If you were to attend a modern theatre performance tonight, you would usually go in the early evening, spend about two hours at the play, and then return home.

Theatre in ancient Greece was an all-day event. During the day, five plays were put on. Ancient Greeks were content to spend the entire day at the theatre. Can you imagine spending a whole day at the theatre?

1. Describe the ancient Greeks' sense of time.
2. How is your sense of time different from the ancient Greek sense of time?
3. Which sense of time do you think you would enjoy the most? Give some reasons for your answer.

Plays were split into three categories: comedies, tragedies, and **satyrs**. The plays were based on myths and legends. They were held in honour of the gods during religious festivals. At the plays, prizes were awarded by judges for the best plays each year. Winning an award at the Greater Dionysia in the spring was a special honour.

The greatest playwrights in ancient Greece were Aeschylus, Sophocles, Euripides, and Aristophanes. The first three men wrote tragedies and the fourth wrote comedies.

 **KEY CONCEPTS**

Theatre is a form of entertainment in many cultures. Theatre tells stories about the culture and provides enjoyment for the people who watch it. Theatre has played an important role throughout history.

Famous Playwrights of Ancient Greece

Aeschylus (525-456 BC) wrote plays that showed his characters as heroes but human. He wrote a trilogy, called the *Oresteia*. It is about Agamemnon returning from Troy, being murdered by his wife Clytemnestra, and the subsequent revenge by his son Orestes. Aeschylus introduced the idea of a second actor into a play.

Sophocles (496-406 BC) was one of ancient Greece's greatest playwrights. His characters were very noble. His most famous play was called *Oedipus Rex* or *Oedipus the King*. Sophocles introduced a third actor and background scene paintings.

Euripides (485-406 BC) wrote plays showing characters who behaved more as ordinary humans than as heroes. He introduced romance into plays and tried to show women's feelings accurately.

Aristophanes (450-385 BC) wrote comedies about famous people (such as Socrates) and events (such as the wars with Sparta).

KEY FACTS

Music can encourage, relax, and allow people to express themselves in a society. The people of ancient Greece used music to celebrate special events, to entertain, and for relaxation. Many of the great poems of Homer were sung to music. These provided hours of enjoyment for the ancient Greeks.

WHAT WAS MUSIC LIKE IN ANCIENT GREECE?

Music was important to the ancient Greeks, and they enjoyed it very much. It was often included at an after-dinner party (symposium). The most popular instruments were the lyre (hand-held harp) and the double flute (pan pipes).

The flute was considered the poor man's music, but the lyre was considered to be music fit for people of status. The ancient Greeks also used drums and horns. Drums were used on ritual occasions and were exotic to the ancient Greeks. Horns were used for military purposes, not entertainment.

KEY FACTS

The ancient Greeks invented many early musical instruments and musical styles. Although these differ from music today, they helped us develop the music we enjoy. The great Greek mathematician, Pythagoras, first discovered the octave (eight notes on a scale). Ask your music teacher about this if you don't know what this means.

One reason the ancient Greeks liked music was that it helped them remember their poetry. Like today, music and poetry were put together. At school, young men learned to recite poetry accompanied by the lyre. It was much like singing along to a guitar. When the ancient Greeks recited the *Iliad* and the *Odyssey*, they were accompanied by music.

Music and singing were done at festivals, at dramatic events, at weddings, or even when training warriors. Words such as *chorus* and *orchestra*, and even *music*, came from the Greek language.

• *The ancient Greeks loved music. One of their favourite musical instruments was the lyre.*
• *Write a brief description of this musical instrument.*
• *Is the lyre a common instrument today? What instruments are similar to the lyre?*

• *Many ancient Greeks learned how to play the double flute.*
• *Look at this picture and tell how the double flute made music.*
• *What musical instruments do we have today that ancient Greeks would not have seen? Which instruments would be the most confusing to them?*

What Do Music and Math Have in Common?

Math and music both begin with the letter m, but what else do they have in common? Did you know that most music is mathematical? The great Greek mathematician, Pythagoras, first discovered the octave. But not all music is based on the same mathematical ideas. Therefore, music from different parts of the world can sound very different.

WRAPPING UP

1. Why did actors in ancient Greece wear masks?
2. (a) Draw a picture of an ancient Greek theatre. Base your drawing on the information in the chapter. Under your picture, create a caption that describes what you have drawn.
   (b) How was ancient Greek theatre different from dramatic entertainment today (including theatre and television)?
3. What role did music play in ancient Greece? What role does it play in our society today?
4. (a) Using the glossary, look up comedy and tragedy. What are the differences between the two?
   (b) List three of your favourite books, television shows, or stories. Beside each choice, identify whether it is usually a comedy or a tragedy.
5. Compose a short, one-page play about life in ancient Greece. You may choose any characters or activities you want. Try to base your play on information that might have been true in that society. There are many possibilities. Some suggestions are the actions of the gods or goddesses on human life, a slave being welcomed into a new family, or a war scene between Persians and Greeks.
6. Would you have enjoyed theatre in ancient Greece? Choose some things you might have liked and some parts you might not have liked. List them in a simple chart.

DEVELOPING YOUR SKILLS

1. Design a playbill or poster advertising upcoming plays during the Greater Dionysia. Include the price, the name of the play, the playwright's name, where it was being held, and when. Draw a scene from the play on the poster. Imagine this poster in the agora.
2. Look at the drawings of Greek masks in your textbook. Draw or make papier-mache masks showing tragic or comic features.

MOVING ON

In this chapter, you learned that theatre and music were both ways that ancient Greeks expressed themselves. They met their psychological needs by going to the theatre, and listening to or playing music. They entertained themselves.

To the ancient Greeks (and to us) entertainment provided a time to relax after a busy day. But psychological needs include more than just relaxation. Religion was important to the ancient Greeks. Many ancient Greeks met psychological needs by practising their religion, and many of us do the same today. The next chapter will help you understand how the ancient Greeks practised their religion. You will learn that, in many ways, their religion was very different from religious practices today.

Religion in Ancient Greece

DIGGING UP

1. Write definitions for "myth" and "legend." Do you know any myths or legends? If so, briefly describe one.
2. As you read this chapter, "dig up" ways that stories and tales about gods and goddesses helped the ancient Greeks meet their needs.

WHAT RELIGIOUS BELIEFS DID THE ANCIENT GREEKS HAVE?

PEOPLE in ancient Greece were very religious. They did not share the same religious beliefs we have today. To the ancient Greeks, the gods and goddesses helped explain natural forces they did not fully understand. They told many stories and tales about their gods and goddesses. Many of these survive today as legends and myths.

If you visit the temples the ancient Greeks built, you will understand how much they respected and feared their gods and goddesses. They believed that the deities were often angered by human actions and would punish humans for what they did. Zeus was their chief god. He lived with the other gods and goddesses on Mount Olympus.

KEY CONCEPTS

Each society develops its own belief and value systems. These beliefs and values can be seen in how people act and in what they hold as valuable in their lives. Each civilization places different values on different things. These values are a society's way of showing what it thinks is important in life.

Like many cultures, the ancient Greeks had their own theory of how the world was created. Early Greeks believed that before the Earth formed there was Chaos, a word meaning void. Later, after the rule of gods called Titans, the Olympians led by Zeus became the next generation of gods and goddesses. The ancient Greeks worshipped these deities.

Ancient Greek gods and goddesses had human forms. The people prayed to them for help and for favours. To please the gods and goddesses, ancient Greeks brought them gifts of food and art. They also sacrificed animals to the gods and goddesses for their help.

A Poem About the Gods

In an earlier chapter, we met Hesiod, the poet who lived about 700 BC in Boeotia. Why the gods would come to him, he did not know. But they did come, he claimed, and their directions were specific. Sing about the things to come, and the things that had been, and about the eternal gods. So, Hesiod sang his poetry.

One of Hesiod's poems was about the gods and how they acted. He organized and wrote the greatest history of the gods. This work was called the *Theogony*. In the *Theogony*, Hesiod explained that Zeus ruled the world and was the god of justice. Zeus controlled the destiny of all humans. Zeus and the other gods often came to Earth to give and to take from humanity — as they willed.

Hesiod's poetry did not paint a pretty picture. Humans were going from bad to worse. Eventually, Zeus would destroy them.

Until Zeus destroyed the world, good humans would prosper. Zeus would reward them with peace and good harvests. In his anger, Zeus would reward wicked people differently. They would be given famine, plague, and war.

What should people do when faced with an angry god such as Zeus? Hesiod offered some practical advice. They should be careful farmers. If they were good farmers, they would have good harvests. Then they could afford to be just and kind.

WHO WERE SOME GREEK GODS AND GODDESSES?

The following are descriptions of the more well-known ancient Greek deities.

Zeus ruled all the gods on Mount Olympus. He was the lord of the sky and sent rain, wind, and the dew. He was the god of justice. His symbol was the thunderbolt.

Hera was Zeus' wife. She protected marriages and the home.

Poseidon was Zeus' brother and god of the sea. His symbol was the trident.

Hades was the brother of Zeus and Poseidon. He ruled the underworld and the dead.

Athena was Zeus' daughter. She was the goddess of wisdom and of strategy in war. Her symbols were the olive tree and the owl.

Apollo was Zeus' son. He was the god of shepherds and of music. His symbols were the lyre and the laurel tree.

Artemis was Apollo's twin sister. She was the goddess of light, the moon, maidens, and of the hunt. Her symbol was the bow.

Aphrodite was the goddess of beauty and love. She was the wife of Ares.

• *The ancient Greeks believed in many different gods and goddesses.*
• *Each god and goddess was known for different things. Look at the symbols and read the text to identify the deities in this picture.*
• *What do these symbols tell you about the traits of these deities?*

Hermes was Zeus' son. He was the messenger of the gods and guided souls to the underworld. He carried a winged staff.

Ares was the son of Zeus and Hera. He was the god of war. He was murderous and was hated by the gods.

Hephaestus was the son of Zeus and Hera. He was the god of fire and artisans. He was the blacksmith of the gods. His symbols were the hammer and tongs.

Hestia was Zeus' sister. She was the goddess of the hearth and home.

Dionysus was the god of wine and vegetation. Women worshipped him in secret rites.

Demeter was Zeus' sister. She was the goddess of the Earth. She had a daughter named Persephone.

HOW DID RELIGIOUS BELIEFS AFFECT PEOPLE'S LIVES?

The ancient Greeks believed oracles could foresee the future and tell them the will of the gods. The oracle at Delphi was the **sacred** shrine of Apollo. People often consulted the priestess there for signs from the gods. Goats were sacrificed at Delphi and then the purified priestess consulted the gods. The priestess of Apollo at Delphi was called the Pythia.

Homes in ancient Greece had their own altars to the gods and goddesses. Most courtyards in the homes had a small altar where private sacrifices could be made to the gods. People asked for wealth, health, and safety. There were many religious festivals all over Greece and temples and shrines to honour the deities.

The Oracle at Delphi

High on the steep slopes of Mount Parnassus sat a temple. This temple was no ordinary temple. It was the temple of Apollo where ancient Greeks could consult the oracle of Delphi.

When ancient Greeks had a problem or needed advice, they knew where to go. Straight to the oracle at Delphi. No Greek city-state would consider going to war without consulting the oracle. Nor would an ancient Greek be foolish enough to undertake anything important without a word from the gods.

Greeks from all over the peninsula brought their questions to the oracle. Before seeing the oracle, they would buy or find a goat to sacrifice. When they arrived, the procedure was easy to follow.

First, a priest sprinkled the goat with water. Second, the goat was watched. If the goat didn't shiver, it was a sign that it did not agree to be sacrificed, and the god Apollo would not speak. However, if the goat shivered, this meant the goat agreed to be sacrificed. If the goat shivered, it was sacrificed.

Third, the question the ancient Greek wanted answered was written down and taken inside by the priests. Inside, the note would be read to a special priestess, called the Pythia, who sat in a trance upon a golden tripod. After the question was asked of the priestess, she would respond. Her response, either words or moaning, would be written down by the priests.

Fourth, the priests would return to the questioner and interpret the sayings or moanings. As a way to "influence" the correct answer, the smart Greek would bring special gifts to the oracle. Sometimes people who had prospered by the oracle's advice on other occasions would be asked to bring the gifts.

 **KEY FACTS** Ancient Greek religious life met psychological and social needs. It helped people know how to conduct themselves in their daily lives. It also helped people know what was expected of them in their daily activities.

- *The Pythia at Delphi gave advice to ancient Greeks who wanted to know the will of the gods.*
- *What advice might the Pythia give to a leader in ancient Greece?*
- *What part did the Pythia play in the religious beliefs of the ancient Greeks?*

WRAPPING UP

1. What was the name of the chief god of ancient Greece? Where did he live?
2. Write three things the ancient Greeks believed about their gods and goddesses.
3. Create a matching test to give to a classmate. On this test, write questions about the gods and goddesses that are matched to a description of each.
4. Who are your favourite three gods? Why did you choose them?
5. How were the ancient Greek ideas about religion similar to yours? How are they different?
6. (a) Why do you think that the ancient Greeks believed the stories about the gods and goddesses?
   (b) Do you find any parts of the stories of the ancient Greek gods and goddesses believable? Why or why not?

DEVELOPING YOUR SKILLS

1. Find a book on ancient Greek myths. Choose one myth. Create a modern-day myth that uses the same plot as the myth you chose. Read your story to a friend. See if he or she can tell which ancient myth you were using.
2. Research and write a summary of one of the following deities: Themis, Pan, Dionysus, Helios, Asclepius, or Selene.
3. Create a mural depicting the gods and goddesses on Mount Olympus.
4. Create a cartoon or poster that shows one of the ancient Greek myths.

MOVING ON

In this chapter you learned about the religion of the ancient Greeks. You learned that the ancient Greeks believed in many gods and goddesses. You also learned that the ancient Greeks believed that the gods could be consulted about important questions.

Like many people today, the ancient Greeks held their religious beliefs strongly. They believed that worshipping the gods should be taken seriously. If you visit Greece today, you can see just how seriously the ancient Greeks took their religion. You will see the remains of the great buildings that the ancient Greeks built as houses for their gods and goddesses. You will see the statues that sculptors spent many years creating in honour of their gods and goddesses.

Studying the building and architecture of ancient Greek temples can help us understand the people's religious practices and their architecture. In the next chapter, you will learn what the buildings of ancient Greece were like. You will also learn how they were built. As you read, think about how we construct buildings today for religious practice. Think also about the role buildings play in religion today.

Temples in Ancient Greece

DIGGING UP
1. What is a temple? What are the different kinds of temples found in your community? Describe what one of the temples in your area looks like.
2. Look at the picture of the Parthenon and read the descriptions of ancient Greek temples. As you read this chapter, "dig up" ways that temples in your country are similar and different from the ones in ancient Greece.

WHY DID THE ANCIENT GREEKS BUILD TEMPLES?

TEMPLES were an important part of the religious practices of the ancient Greeks. Temples were the homes of their gods and goddesses. Temples were filled with beautiful sculptures. The sailors and merchants who went far from Greece brought home jewellery, **trinkets** of gold, and many things made of ivory. Many of these were placed in the temples for the gods and goddesses.

**KEY CONCEPTS**   Temples were important to ancient civilizations. Even today religious buildings are important. They provide a place for people to meet and share their beliefs.

Temples in ancient Greece were usually simple in design. Most were rectangular. The support pillars for the temples were huge columns of marble. These columns rested on large stone platforms. Even though the marble columns were huge, the decoration at the top of them could be intricate. Columns were typically topped with one of three different styles of **capitals**: Doric, Ionic, or Corinthian. As well, decorated sculpture often ran in horizontal bands above the columns.

If you ever have a chance to visit Athens, take a close look at the Parthenon. You would probably be struck by two thoughts. First, this ancient Greek temple is very beautiful. Second, it is very large. It is inspiring to think that the ancient Greeks could build and then move the giant, heavy stones and columns that make up their temples.

WHAT IS THE PARTHENON?

The Parthenon is the most famous temple in Greece. At the Parthenon, the ancient Greeks worshipped the goddess Athena. Worshipping was done at the entrance to the temple. It was never done inside. The inside of the temple belonged to the goddess Athena. Behind the room housing the statue of Athena was a treasury room to house the offerings that were collected.

The Parthenon was rebuilt in the time of Pericles on the Acropolis of Athens after the Persians burned the original Parthenon in 480 BC. Construction on the new Parthenon began in 447 BC. The Parthenon was built from marble brought from Mount Pentelikos near Athens.

DORIC   IONIC   CORINTHIAN

• *The ancient Greeks used three types of columns for their buildings.*
• *Describe the differences between these three types of columns. Which do you prefer? Why?*
• *Does ancient Greek architecture still influence our modern buildings? Do buildings around you have columns designed like these Greek columns? If so, which buildings?*

• *The remains of the Parthenon attract many visitors to Athens today.*
• *Look at this picture and the one of the Acropolis on pages 8 and 9 of this book. Where is the Parthenon located on the Acropolis? Why?*
• *Compare the size of the Parthenon to the other buildings on the Acropolis. Is it bigger or smaller? Try to explain why.*

WHAT WERE SOME OTHER BUILDINGS ON THE ACROPOLIS?

Many people hear the term acropolis and wonder what this building looked like. But the acropolis was not a building at all. It was the name given to the high hill around which an ancient Greek city-state was built.

Remember that Greece is mountainous. When the ancient Greeks began to build a community, they chose wisely. They knew they would probably be attacked sooner or later, so they chose a site that could be protected. This site was the highest point of an area — the acropolis.

The acropolis was a position that could be defended against invaders. The acropolis was also the site chosen for temples. To the ancient Greeks, these hilltop sites were the homes of the gods. They provided a place of **sanctuary**.

If you were to visit the Parthenon today, its empty shell would tell you much about the beauty of the temple's design. However, much of the temple has been destroyed. What you would see is the outer structure of a busy place of Greek worship. You would not see the huge gold and ivory statue of Athena. Nor would you see the inner chambers and **porticos**. The statue of Athena was destroyed in ancient times. The inner chambers were ruined about 300 years ago.

• *The Erechtheum is another temple found on the Acropolis of Athens.*
• *Compare the Erechtheum to the Parthenon. In what ways do they look the same? In what ways do they look different?*
• *Why do you think the people of Athens built more than one temple on the Acropolis?*

⚷ KEY FACTS

To meet their psychological needs, ancient Greeks built temples. These temples were part of their religious practice. Today we still enjoy and marvel at the beauty of these buildings. In fact, many designs from ancient Greece are used today in the design of buildings.

The Acropolis of Athens is a rocky hill near the centre of the city. Athenians built their most sacred temples on the Acropolis. From the Acropolis, Athenians can see the entire Bay of Salamis and part of the Aegean Sea beyond. If invaders were moving in for an attack, the Athenians would have plenty of time to take action.

Despite erosion, invasion, and the removal of their treasures, many buildings from Athens' Acropolis still survive. One of these is the temple called the Erechtheum. This building contained the most holy of all statues of Athena.

Another surviving structure on the Acropolis of Athens is the Propylaea, the huge entrance to the Acropolis. Another small temple, that of Athena Nike (which means "victory"), still stands near the Propylaea.

• The small Temple of Athena Nike stands near the entrance to the Acropolis.
• Look closely at this temple. Are its columns Doric, Ionic, or Corinthian?
• Do any buildings today look similar to the Athena Nike?

 WRAPPING UP

1. (a) What type of columns were built in the Parthenon?
   (b) Why was it such an important place?
2. (a) Draw a picture of the Parthenon.
   (b) Write a caption for this picture that gives at least one important fact about it.
3. Draw a column and label the various parts. Search through pictures of modern buildings, or look at local architecture, until you find a building with columns like these. Can you find a column in buildings around where you live?
4. (a) What is an acropolis?
   (b) Why do you think the ancient Greeks found it important to use an acropolis? Give two reasons.
5. Compare the Parthenon to the Temple of Athena Nike. What are some differences? What are some similarities?
6. Why do you think the ancient Greeks built many of their temples on higher ground? Do we build certain buildings in special places? Why?

DEVELOPING YOUR SKILLS

1. Research the construction of the Parthenon. As part of your research, make sure to find out how Pheidias created optical illusions when he and other architects built the Parthenon.
2. Look at the picture of the three different types of columns used in the temples of ancient Greece. Cut out or construct columns and match capitals to columns. Label the type of column and its various parts.

 MOVING ON

In this chapter, you learned about some great buildings of ancient Greece. You learned how they were built, what they were built from, the purposes they served, and how they helped the Greeks meet their psychological needs. But so far your study has left out one of the most famous aspects of ancient Greek culture — the Olympics. No study of ancient Greece would be complete without looking at this area.

The next chapter discusses the place of the Olympics in ancient Greece. As you study about the Olympic games, try to think about how they helped the ancient Greeks meet their psychological needs. You will learn how the Olympics started, how they grew, and what they mean to us today.

The Olympics in Ancient Greece

DIGGING UP

1. Have you ever seen the Olympics or watched the Olympics on television? What is your favourite Olympic event?
2. As you read this chapter, "dig up" some ancient Greek beliefs and values that the Olympics has brought to Western civilization.

HOW DID THE OLYMPICS BEGIN?

IN ancient times, one of the Seven Wonders of the World was located fifteen kilometres from the mouth of the Alpheus River on the Ionian Sea. This ancient wonder was the statue of Zeus sculpted by Pheidias from gold and ivory. The statue no longer exists, but we have representations of it on coins from ancient Greece.

On the right bank of the Alpheus River, archaeologists have dug up the remains of great temples. One of these temples would have housed Pheidias' statue of Zeus. The archaeologists have also found a large stadium and an ancient statue of Hermes on this river bank.

What is this place? What happened here? The place is ancient Olympia, the site where the first Olympic games were held. Many myths and stories tell about the first Olympic games.

One myth says that the first Olympic contest was a chariot race between the King of Pisa and Pelops. As the early Olympics grew, new legends were told about their beginnings. Zeus, father-god of the Dorians, became the protector of the stadium. Herakles, Zeus' son, became the founder of the games. Before long, any legend that did not have Zeus and Herakles as heroes was rejected.

• *Olympic athletes in ancient Greece trained very hard. These athletes are training in a gymnasium.*
• *What events are these athletes training for?*
• *What events from the ancient Olympics are still part of our modern games? What events are new? Read on in the chapter to find out.*

Herakles

Herakles was a legendary Greek hero. If you see drawings of him, he is usually wearing a lion skin and carrying a club. He was known for his strength and courage.

Herakles was the son of Zeus. But Herakles was a human, not a god. Hera, Zeus' wife, hated Herakles. She tried to kill him by putting snakes in his cradle, but he killed the snakes. Later, Hera sent a fit of madness on Herakles and forced him to kill his wife and children. Herakles became the servant of Eurystheus. As a servant, he was forced to complete 12 labours.

Finishing these 12 labours made Herakles famous. He killed the lion of Nemea and the nine-headed Hydra. He captured the Erymanthean boar and the golden-antlered Cerynean hind. He destroyed the dangerous Stymphalian birds. He cleaned the Augean stables by changing the course of two rivers so they would flow through the stables. He captured the Cretan bull and the man-eating horses of Thrace. He stole the Amazon Queen's girdle, the cattle of Geryon, and the golden apples of the Hesperides. And, last, he brought Cerberus out of Hades.

The legend of Herakles shows how humans believed the gods worked in their lives. The gods controlled human life, but they were not always very kind. They tricked humans. They forced them into madness.

You may know of Herakles by his Roman name, Hercules.

• In Greek mythology, Herakles completed several tests of strength.
• What can you see in the picture of Herakles that would suggest he was a mighty hunter?
• What labours did Herakles perform? Which one would have been the most difficult?

In ancient Greece, religious festivals were the main means of entertainment. The Olympic games are a legacy of the ancient Greeks.

In 776 BC, the first true Olympic games were held. The birth date of those first Olympic games became the first year of the Olympiad calendar. This calendar was used by many ancient writers. The games were held every four years at Olympia as a festival to honour the god Zeus.

During the Olympics, Greeks came from all over the ancient world to worship their gods and goddesses. On the ancient Olympic grounds stood the Temple of Zeus. Inside this temple was the statue of Zeus. Many people who visited Olympia came to worship at the altar of Zeus. When they worshipped, they

• *The entrance to the stadium at Olympia was so narrow that only a few athletes could enter at one time. The inset picture is a starting line, made of stones.*
• *The ancient Greeks built each part of the stadium for a particular reason. How might the entrance to the stadium have encouraged the crowd to react?*
• *Use another resource book to find out what some Olympic stadiums look like today.*

placed gifts to Zeus around the stadium. Some Greek cities and colonies established treasuries here to honour the gods and goddesses and gain recognition for themselves.

Olympia's fame grew. As it did, Olympia had many visitors. New sports were added to the games. The Olympic games were a test of strength. For example, one event tested which competitor could run the fastest in hoplite armour. Legend tells us that the first winner of an Olympic foot race was Corybos from Elis. Foot races were one stadion (about 185 metres) long. By 384 BC, there were 18 Olympic events.

The events in these ancient games were both similar to and different from events in the modern Olympics. For example, both modern and ancient Olympics include the long jump. In ancient Greece, however, a competitor in the long jump carried weights in his hands for more momentum. Other events included javelin throwing, the discus, wrestling, boxing, and a violent combination of wrestling and boxing called pankration.

The **pentathlon** was the most important event of the Olympics. It included five events: the long jump, discus, javelin, wrestling, and the 185 metre dash. The winner of this event was thought to be one of the best athletes in the world.

The games were open to athletes from any city-state. But, unlike the modern Olympic games, the ancient Olympics barred women and non-Greeks from competition.

Like today's Olympic games, the ancient Greeks believed that their games should be peaceful. A **truce** between warring Greek city-states was called. During this truce, all fighting stopped. No death sentences were executed. No problems were discussed. To ancient Greeks, worshipping Zeus was very important. To break the Olympic truce meant never to be admitted into Olympia. It also meant punishment by Zeus. This truce helped the ancient Greek city-states become more unified because, for a short time, they quit fighting and celebrated together. This truce also made it possible for athletes and spectators to cross warring areas and reach Olympia safely.

• The discus was part of the early Olympic games. It is still an Olympic event.
• What does the athlete's wreath signify?
• Find out more about the discus event in the Olympics. Is this event the same today as it was in ancient times? Explain.

> ⊙—KEY CONCEPTS
>
> The Olympics have played an important role through the centuries. The early games were dedicated to the worship of gods and goddesses. Today the Olympics are a sports event. Countries from around the world compete in the Olympics.

The tradition of **amateur** competition has been carried down from the first Olympic games. In these ancient games, the winners received a wild olive wreath, nothing more. Winners were treated like **celebrities** in their city-states. Many received free meals for life and were given front-row seats at plays. Statues were often erected in their honour.

Like sporting events today, the first Olympic games had concession booths. Spectators could buy wine and fruit just as we buy hot dogs and soft drinks.

In the 4th century AD, the Olympic games were abolished by the Christian emperor Theodosius I.

WHAT DO THE MODERN OLYMPICS OWE THE ANCIENT GREEKS?

The modern Olympics come from these ancient religious practices. In the modern Olympics, however, sports has become the most important part of the festival. The modern Olympic games are an athletic competition. They are held every four years. The games are separated into two parts: the Winter Olympics and the Summer Olympics. The first modern summer games were held in Athens, Greece, in 1896. The winter games began in 1924 in France. Women first competed in the Olympic games in 1912.

Although the Olympic contestants represent countries, they win individual medals. All events are given three medals. A gold medal is awarded for a first place finish, a silver medal for a second place finish, and a bronze medal for a third place finish.

The Olympic games today are amateur competitions. Though some athletes are professionals, they are not paid for competing in the Olympic games.

Today's Olympic games are a constant reminder of the debt modern societies owe to the ancient Greeks.

 WRAPPING UP

1. (a) Why did the ancient Greeks celebrate the Olympics? What festivals do we celebrate today that are similar to those practised by the ancient Greeks?
   (b) When were the modern Olympics started?
2. (a) Make a list of the events in the modern Olympics. (You may use an encyclopedia for help.)
   (b) Make a list of the events in the ancient Olympics.
   (c) Compare the two lists. Why do you think there are similarities and differences?
3. What is the purpose of the Olympic games today?
4. Do we treat Olympic athletes as heroes today? Do we treat other athletes as heroes? Name a few of your favourite athletes and explain what sport they play and why they are important.
5. (a) Consider the Olympic games from an athlete's point of view. Do the ancient games and the modern Olympics demand a different kind of training?

(b) Did the ancient games demand different athletic abilities than the modern games?

6. (a) Do you think there is too much emphasis on athletes as heroes today? Are athletes paid too much, in both praise and money, for what they do?

(b) Should professional athletes be allowed to compete in the Olympic games? Would this conflict with the nature of the games? Why or why not?

DEVELOPING YOUR SKILLS

1. (Art) Design a poster for the next Olympic games. Before you design this poster, think about what should be included. When do the next Olympics take place? What events will be included? Who does the Olympics honour? Where will the next Olympics be held?

2. Pretend you are a sports columnist with a newspaper in ancient Greece (you name the paper). Write an account of an event at the Olympic games.

MOVING ON

In this chapter, you learned that the Olympics started as a religious festival and later became known as a sports event. You also learned that the modern Olympics have roots in ancient Olympia. Now that you know more about the Olympics, you can watch them in a different light. For example, if you watch the Olympic pentathlon, you may be reminded of the origins of the event.

You have read of the many ways ancient Greeks left their mark on civilization today. You know that ancient Greeks met their physical, social and psychological needs better than other groups at the time. But what caused their fall as the greatest civilization of their time? How could a society that was so strong become weak and be conquered? That is what you will find out in the next section.

PART V

The Decline of Ancient Greece

You have almost completed your study of ancient Greece. In the next chapter, you will study the final days of the civilization of ancient Greece. You will learn about the leadership of one man — Alexander the Great. You will see that any society can become weak.

You will also tie together all the things you have learned in this book. You will consider all the information you have found on your archaeological dig.

18

Alexander the Great and Ancient Greece

DIGGING UP

1. Name one great leader in the history of your country. Write a paragraph describing what made that leader great.
2. Alexander the Great became the ruler of ancient Greece when he was only 20 years old. As you read this chapter, "dig up" reasons Alexander was called "the Great." What happened to his empire after he died?

WHO WAS ALEXANDER THE GREAT?

IN 356 BC, a boy named Alexander was born. In 338 BC, Alexander's father, Philip of Macedonia, conquered Greece. A couple of years later, just before his armies were to invade Persia, Philip was murdered. The boy, Alexander, became king. He was 20 years of age.

 **KEY CONCEPTS**

Every civilization has great leaders. These leaders are known for what they accomplish. If a civilization is to prosper, it must continue to produce such people.

Philip of Macedonia had admired and copied Greek ideas and customs. Like most fathers, he believed that Alexander should be well educated. So Philip found the best teacher available at the time. This teacher's name was Aristotle.

As you read earlier, Aristotle was a famous Greek **scholar** and one of the greatest teachers of all time. Among the things Alexander learned from Aristotle was a love for Greek customs and ideas. As Alexander's armies conquered the ancient world, Alexander spread Greek culture and ideas.

Although Alexander was young, he knew how to win battles. When the Greek city-state of Thebes revolted against Macedonian rule, Alexander destroyed the whole city. This made people in the other city-states think twice about fighting Alexander's armies.

Winning battles throughout the Greek peninsula was an accomplishment for a young person of 20. But Alexander didn't stop with Greece. The rest of the world lay ahead of him. He quickly turned his armies against the mighty empire of Persia, in Asia Minor.

In 333 BC, at the Battle of Issus, Alexander defeated the Persian King Darius III. Next he marched to Egypt. Here he founded Alexandria. His armies pushed deeper into Persia, where he fought and defeated Darius again at Gaugamela in 331 BC. In a short time, Alexander's armies controlled Greece, Egypt, and the whole Persian Empire.

By the age of 29, Alexander had pushed his army into what is now India. Here the fighting ended. It wasn't that his armies were defeated. Nor had Alexander reached the end of his military goals. Instead, his soldiers had grown tired of war. They had marched and fought for seven years! Alexander turned back.

In 327 BC, Alexander married a Persian woman named Roxanne, whom he had captured at Oxyartes. His marriage to a Persian woman made his followers unhappy. Many of his Macedonian soldiers felt that Alexander was adopting too many Persian customs and forgetting his Greek ideals. For example, he took many wives, which his soldiers did not like.

Alexander's armies were finished conquering the world, but his task was not over. Alexander worked to bring all the territory he had

- *Alexander the Great had one of the best teachers of all time. His name was Aristotle.*
- *How does the classroom in this picture differ from yours? Which would you prefer?*
- *From what you know about Aristotle, what do you think he taught Alexander?*

The Empire of Alexander the Great

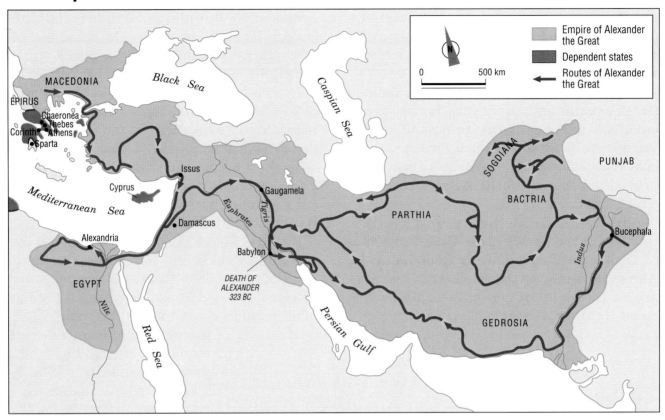

• *This map shows Alexander the Great's empire at the time of his death in 323* BC.
• *Using the scale, calculate the distance from Athens to Bucephala.*
• *Compare this map to a modern map of the world. What modern countries now exist where Alexander once ruled? What does your answer to this question and the previous one tell you about the size of Alexander's empire?*

 KEY FACTS   **The spread of Greek culture was a result of Alexander the Great's conquests. Alexander was one of the most famous leaders in the history of the world.**

won in battle under one government. He might have succeeded, but he caught a fever. In 323 BC, at the age of 32, Alexander died.

In 12 years, Alexander the Great had conquered an enormous territory. He was legend in his lifetime, one of the world's earliest celebrities. His body was buried in a golden coffin in the city named after him, Alexandria, in Egypt.

There was not another leader like Alexander the Great for a long time. After his death, his empire split into several sections. By 303 BC, small pieces of his empire were controlled by his generals. These generals fought each other for control. The empire became weak. It was eventually conquered by the strong, new army of Rome. Greece and other parts of Alexander's empire became Roman provinces.

• As Alexander the Great marched his army into India, he faced an enemy who rode elephants.
• How effective do you think elephants would be in a battle? Look at the drawing. Where do you think is the safest place?
• Review Alexander's march across the ancient world. When did he invade India? Why might Alexander have wanted to invade India?

The Legend of Bucephalus

Bucephalus was one of the largest and blackest horses that Philip had ever seen. But it was the white mark on its forehead and the horse's spirit that attracted Alexander's father. No one could ride Bucephalus. It was just too wild.

Finally, in despair, Philip gave up and told the horse trader to lead Bucephalus away. But Alexander, who was 12, protested. At first Philip told Alexander that he could not have the horse, but offered him a challenge. If Alexander could ride the horse, he could have it. The horse would be his.

Alexander was very clever. He had noticed that the horse was spooked by its own shadow. Quickly, he took the horse's lead and turned it to face the sun. Bucephalus soon quieted down, and when it did Alexander jumped on its back. The great black horse ran wildly for a short time, with young Alexander hanging on.

Soon Bucephalus calmed down. When Philip saw what Alexander had done, he proudly kept his word to his son. Bucephalus and Alexander remained together for many years, marching across the world.

- *After Alexander the Great tamed the mighty horse Bucephalus, they travelled the ancient world together.*
- *Look at this picture of Alexander the Great. What is the artist trying to tell you about his personality?*
- *Did horses help soldiers win battles?*

HOW DID THE GREEK CULTURE SURVIVE AFTER ALEXANDER THE GREAT?

> **The Hellenistic Period shows the powerful influence of Greece on the Roman Empire and in Egypt.**

An important point to remember about Alexander was that, wherever he went, he spread Greek culture and ideas. Today, whenever people move from one place to another, they also bring their ideas and way of life with them.

Eventually, Alexander's empire fell apart. Many parts of it were ruled by Rome. But the people Alexander had conquered adopted and kept many Greek ideas as part of the way they lived.

Ptolemy

Ptolemy was the name of a Greek general. It was also the name of a **dynasty** of 14 kings who ruled Egypt for 300 years. Ptolemy I was one of Alexander the Great's best generals.

When Alexander died, Ptolemy I took control of Egypt. After a long fight, in 305 BC Ptolemy I named himself "king." He was a strong ruler. He built Alexandria into a great business and cultural centre. His son, Ptolemy II, was an even better ruler than Ptolemy I. Under his leadership, Egypt became a great power.

The remaining 12 Ptolemys were not good leaders. Their rule was filled with murder and corruption. They ruled poorly until the time of Cleopatra in 30 BC, when Egypt became a province of Rome.

After Alexander the Great died, his generals fought to control his empire. The generals feared each other. They also feared Roxanne, Alexander's widow, and her young son. Because they believed that Roxanne and Alexander's son might try to rule, the generals had them killed.

Eventually, Alexander's empire was split among the strongest generals. One general named Seleucus gained control of Persia. His family stayed in control for more than two centuries. Ptolemy I, another powerful general, gained control of Egypt. One of Ptolemy's descendants was Cleopatra, famous queen of Egypt.

> **In all civilizations, people contribute to the overall knowledge, art, or technology of the society. These contributions help the society to prosper. Many of those who contributed to Greek society have also affected Western civilization.**

The strength of Greek culture did not decline with its military power. In Alexandria, the first museum and library was opened. This library contained many books written by Greek writers. This library was so large it became one of the Seven Wonders of the World. It contained many books about early Greek literature.

Thousands of Greeks settled in Egypt. Wherever the Greeks moved, they brought their belongings and their culture. They taught the Egyptians many things. The Greek culture became an important part of Egyptian life. For Egyptians to succeed, they had to speak the Greek language and know the Greek culture.

WRAPPING UP

1. Who was Alexander the Great?
2. How did education influence Alexander's life?
3. How was Alexander the Great different from leaders in your country?
4. Alexander the Great spread the Greek culture throughout the ancient world. How did he do it?
5. Why do you think Alexander wanted to keep adding to his empire when his soldiers wanted to go home?
6. (a) After his death, Alexander the Great's empire was split among his generals. Why do you think this happened?
   (b) Many people believe that a strong ruler helps a country grow stronger. What do you think? Do you think it would be better to live in a democratic country or a country with a strong leader like Alexander the Great?

MOVING ON

In this chapter, you learned about Alexander the Great. You learned how he spread the ancient Greek civilization and what happened to his empire after he died. You also learned that, even though it had been conquered, the ideas of the Greek civilization continued to live and be practised.

These ancient Greeks have influenced the world throughout history. Their contributions to today's way of life remain important. The ancient Greeks worked to meet their own physical, social, and psychological needs. They also helped shape how we meet physical, social, and psychological needs today. The last chapter of your study ties together some of the influences the ancient Greeks have had on today's civilization. The last chapter also ties together the many things you have learned throughout this book.

DEVELOPING YOUR SKILLS

1. Using your imagination or pictures you have found, draw or complete the following:
   (a) a map of Alexander's journeys and conquests (perhaps with a legend showing sites of famous battles)
   (b) coins showing Alexander's likeness
   (c) scenes of battle in India (elephants of King Porus)
   (d) a picture of Philip (Alexander's father)
   (e) a picture of a phalanx and the unusually long spear called a "sarissa"
   (f) a bust of Alexander.
2. Research Alexander's encounter with a man named Diogenes. What was said?

CHAPTER

Conclusion

DIGGING UP

Your archaeological dig is complete. Now is the time to look at everything you have dug up about ancient Greece. Consult your archaeological journal and answer one of the following questions:

1. Choose two of the following topics and write one paragraph each about how the civilization of ancient Greece has influenced Western civilization:
   (a) the Olympics
   (b) architecture
   (c) democracy
   (d) medicine.
2. Do you meet your needs in the same way the ancient Greeks did? Choose one of the following kinds of needs. List similarities and differences between how you meet that need and how the ancient Greeks met that need:
   (a) physical
   (b) social
   (c) psychological needs.

WHAT HAVE YOU LEARNED FROM YOUR STUDY OF ANCIENT GREECE?

We started this book by asking you an important question: "Why do you study ancient Greece?" Are you able to answer this question now, after reading this book? If you did read the book, listened, and thought, then you probably can.

Let us help you review a few important things you have learned.

You learned that the ancient Greeks developed an important civilization more than 3000 years ago. You also learned that this civilization was like yours in many ways. In other ways it was very different. You should now be able to list some of these similarities and differences.

You learned that the ancient Greeks were humans, just like you are. All humans, regardless of when they live, share physical, social, and psychological needs. You also learned that all humans have tried to use their environment to fulfill their needs. The ancient Greeks' homes, education, and religion may have been different, but their needs were very similar to yours.

Probably some things you learned about the ancient Greeks seemed very common to you. For example, it should seem very familiar that the children in ancient Greece learned things, played with toys, and had pets.

Other things you learned about the ancient Greeks might seem strange. For example, ancient Greek worship of gods and goddesses may not be like your religious worship.

Finally, some things you have learned about the ancient Greeks probably seem wrong. Today, people would not agree that young men should go slave hunting just to prove

they are grown up. Today, we do not believe in slavery. We differ from the ancient Greeks in this respect. We believe that all humans should have the right to be free. We do not believe that it is right for one human being to kill another.

Because you have read and studied this book, you should now know much more about ancient Greece than you knew before. How will the information you have learned help you? In a small way, you should be able to recognize some of the many contributions the ancient Greeks have made to your own lives. These contributions are in the areas of drama, architecture, philosophy, education, the Olympics, and government. As you grow, travel, and learn, we encourage you to look for examples of these contributions.

You have also learned a very important lesson about how groups of people can influence each other. You have learned that all groups of people can contribute to the lives of others. You have also learned that it is not always necessary to agree with everything one group believes or how the group acts to appreciate their contributions to your lives. You do not even have to live at the same time.

When you studied the ancient Greek civilization, you studied a civilization that ended a long time ago. The ancient Greeks lived, they grew, they flourished, and their civilization was eventually absorbed by a stronger civilization — the Romans. Yet the lessons of this civilization have had far-reaching effects. You are now able to tell what those effects are. As you do so, you can place the important contributions of ancient Greece into your modern lives.

Maybe the most important thing you have learned is that you are capable young learners. Like the archaeologists and historians

• *Through the centuries, Greeks have worked hard to preserve their heritage. The Temple of Hephaestus in Athens is one of the most well-preserved temples in Greece.*
• *What have you learned about the ancient Greeks by looking at photos and drawings of this and other temples?*
• *Was this temple built to satisfy a physical, social, or psychological need?*

who have studied the ancient civilization of Greece, you too can inquire and learn. You are much more able to ask and answer important questions than you were when you started. You are better able to understand your life than you did before you started.

Throughout this book, you have studied hard. As you studied, you did two things. First, you learned the facts. Second, you learned how to relate to the facts. The questions you answered and the way you answered them will help you become better at exploring other facts and ideas throughout your life.

What will be your next exploration? Perhaps you will study the societies of Italy, France, Germany, Britain, the United States, Canada, Japan, or China. The places you might study are too numerous to list here. Maybe you will be the person who discovers the undersea world of Atlantis. Good luck in your future studies.

Glossary

A

Academic subjects are those concerned with the arts, history, and philosophy. For example, some children in ancient Athens studied academic subjects such as writing, music, and dancing.

The **Academy** was a park near ancient Athens where the philosopher Plato taught. Today, academy refers to a place of instruction or a school where a special subject is studied, such as music or military exercises.

Acid rain is rain that carries chemical substances that can harm buildings, statues, and even people. Acid rain is caused by chemicals such as sulphur dioxide that are created by some industries.

An **acropolis** is a rocky hill, the highest point in a city-state. For example, the ancient Greeks built a fortress on the acropolis to retreat to in times of war.

An **agora** was an outdoor market where shopping and meetings were held. For example, ancient Greek men and women spent time at the agora every day.

An **alkaline** substance is much like soda. For example, some ancient Greeks used a perfumed soap made from an alkaline material.

Alloys are combinations or mixtures of different metals to make other metals. For example, bronze is an alloy made usually by mixing copper and tin.

An **amateur** does an activity for pleasure, not for money. For example, until recently, only amateur athletes could compete at the Olympic games.

Ancient means old, or belonging to times long past. For example, when you study ancient Greece, you are studying a very old civilization.

An **archaeologist's journal** is a diary of notes an archaeologist makes about his or her discoveries. For example, in this book we have asked you to keep your notes in an archaeologist's journal.

Archaeologists study the history and culture of civilizations. For example, archaeologists dig up old cities to find out how that ancient civilization lived.

Archons were judges in the government of Athens. The archons in Athens were elected to run festivals and administer laws.

An **aristocracy** is a ruling class of nobles. Nobles are people with high status within a society. For example, at times ancient Greece was ruled by wealthy families who formed an aristocracy.

Artifacts are objects made by humans. For example, archaeologists dig up a past society's artifacts, or the things that were created by the society.

B

Barracks are buildings where soldiers live and sleep. For example, in ancient Sparta, young men lived in barracks.

Barter is the exchange of goods or services for other goods or services. This exchange is done without using currency.

Bled means that a person has undergone an ancient medical treatment in which his or her body was cut to let the "bad blood" leave it. For example, doctors in ancient Greece bled patients who were ill.

Braziers are open pans for holding hot coals. For example, much of the food in ancient Greece was cooked in open braziers in the courtyard of the home.

The **Bronze Age** is the time in history when bronze was used in the making of tools and weapons. The Bronze Age in ancient Greece took place from about 3000 to 1050 BC.

C

Capitals are the top sections of columns developed in ancient Greece. Today, the word also means the most important city.

Celebrities are famous people. For example, Alexander the Great was one of the world's earliest celebrities.

Chanters were the singers in a chorus who helped tell the story in plays. For example, during a play in ancient Greece, the chanters would stand in the orchestra pit.

A **chiton** was a garment in ancient Greece. For example, some chitons were made from a single sheet of cloth.

A **chlamys** was a short cloak. For example, in ancient Greece, a young person liked to wear a chlamys.

A **citizen** in ancient Greece was a male over the age of 18 who was born in a city-state and so had voting rights there. Slaves and people not born in the city-state were not considered citizens. For example, a male over 18 years old who was born in Athens was a citizen of Athens and could vote there.

A **city-state** was an independent government formed by a city and its surrounding area. For example, most people in ancient Greece lived in city-states.

Civic refers to something related to the city. For example, women in ancient Greece did not have civic rights or responsibilities because they were not allowed to be involved in running the city-state.

A **civilization** is a group of people with distinct social and political organization. A civilization has languages, cultures, laws, traditions and history in common.

The **Classical Period** of ancient Greece, from about 550 to 300 BC, was when Greek art, culture, and thinking were at their peak. For example, most of what we know about ancient Greece comes from the Classical Period.

A **clique** is a group of people with similar interests. For example, ancient Greeks who had high status in the city-state sometimes developed cliques.

Colonists are groups of people who move from their homes to settle and live in another country. For example, in order to trade with other people, ancient Greek colonists explored and set up trading centres.

A **comedy** is a slightly humorous drama about the events of everyday life. For example, comedies in ancient Greece often told the stories of heroes who had problems with the gods and goddesses.

A **constitution** is the basic law of a country. For example, a written constitution tells the people of a country what rights and freedoms they have.

Constitutional law is an area of the law that is concerned with constitutional matters. For example, a constitutional lawyer determines whether a law violates the principles of the constitution.

Context means the circumstances, conditions, or background of a particular event or time. For example, putting the ancient Greeks into context helps us understand why the people lived the way they did.

Conveniences are objects that are designed to make our lives easier. For example, today we have many conveniences the ancient Greeks did not have.

Culture is a term used to describe the beliefs, habits, and institutions of a certain people or community.

Cured means that an animal hide has had the hair, dirt, and meat removed from it through a process involving harsh chemicals. For example, the ancient Greeks cured the hides of cows to make leather.

Currency is another name for money. For example, the drachma was one unit of currency in ancient Greece.

The **customs** of a people are their long-established ways of doing things. For example, when Herodotus travelled around Greece, he observed the customs of other city-states.

Cycladic refers to the group of people who lived on the Cyclades, an island area on the Aegean Sea near Greece, as early as 3000 BC. For example, some of the earliest people of ancient Greece were Cycladic.

D

The **Dark Ages** was a period of history in ancient Greece from about 1050 to 900 BC. We know very little about what happened during the Dark Ages.

A **deity** is a god or goddess. For example, Zeus and Athena were two deities of ancient Greece.

The **Delian League** was an alliance of city-states that paid money to a common treasury to wage war against Persia.

Delicacies are special treats. For example, foods that were only used on special occasions (such as nuts and figs) were delicacies for the ancient Greeks.

A **democracy** is a government elected and controlled by the people.

Denominations are groups or collections of similar items. For example, there are different denominations of currency (such as five and ten dollar bills).

A **dialect** is a form of language used in one particular region or by one particular group of people. For example, the early Greeks belonged to different groups that spoke different dialects.

Differences are characteristics that make people or things unlike each other.

To **dominate** is to control or rule by strength or power. For example, men dominated ancient Greek society by controlling the power in that society.

The **Dorians** were a group of northern Greeks who began to invade the rest of Greece in 1100 BC. The Dorians had iron weapons, which made them stronger than other groups of people in Greece.

Draughts is a game like checkers. For example, ancient Greek children played draughts.

A **dynasty** is a series of rulers or leaders who come from the same family. For example, the Ptolemy family ruled Egypt for 300 years, until Cleopatra's death ended the dynasty.

E

An **epic poem** is a long narrative poem about heroes and their deeds. For example, Homer wrote epic poems that children in ancient Greece studied in school.

Erosion refers to the wearing away of something. For example, soil erosion occurred when ancient civilizations removed the trees that held the soil in place.

To **excavate** is to dig or extract. For example, archaeologists excavate a site by digging up the artifacts.

Exported goods were sent to other countries to be sold. For example, ancient Greece exported olive oil to other civilizations.

F

To receive **favours** meant that a person received special treatment. For example, Olympic athletes in ancient Greece were given special favours.

Fertile land is capable of producing plants or crops. For example, the soil in ancient Greece was not always very fertile.

Festivals are days of feasting and special ceremonies. For example, during festivals, the ancient Greeks worshipped their gods and goddesses by making sacrifices to them.

To **forage** is to search for food or supplies. For example, young Spartan boys were taught to forage and live off the land.

G

A **gymnasium** is a building in which people can exercise or play indoor sports. For example, ancient Greek boys went to the gymnasium to exercise.

H

Harmony is the ability to work or live together. For example, after the ancient Greeks were conquered by the Romans, the two cultures existed in harmony.

Helladic refers to the group of people who lived on the Greek mainland as early as 3000 BC. For example, some of the earliest people in ancient Greece were Helladic.

The **Hellenistic Period** occurred after the Classical Period in ancient Greece. It took place from about 300 to 30 BC. During the Hellenistic Period, Rome grew powerful and conquered ancient Greece.

Helots were slaves in ancient Sparta. Sparta had many Helots.

Heritage refers to the traditions and beliefs passed from generation to generation. For example, much of our heritage comes from the ancient Greeks.

Heroes are people who do great and brave deeds and are admired for them. For example, in Greek mythology, Herakles and Achilles were heroes because of their amazing actions and abilities.

A **himation** was a long cloak. For example, in cool weather ancient Greeks wore a himation over their chiton.

Historians study history. Many historians also write about history. For example, Herodotus, Thucydides, and Xenophon wrote about past events in Greek history.

Hoplites were foot soldiers in ancient Greece. Hoplites carried shields and spears.

I

Imported goods were brought to a country to be sold. For example, tin was imported to ancient Greece from other civilizations.

Imprinted means that an object was stamped. For example, ancient Greek coins were imprinted with pictures of people or animals.

Institutions are accepted laws or ways of doing things. For example, the ancient Greeks believed in the institution of the family.

Interdependence occurs when two or more groups need help from each other. For example, humans are interdependent. They must work together in order to survive.

To be **intoxicated** means to be drunk. For example, people in ancient Greece often drank wine with their meals, but they did not become intoxicated.

Intricate means complex. For example, many columns in ancient Greece architecture had intricate designs.

The **Ionians** were a group of people who lived in central Greece and Asia Minor. Some of the Ionians made many contributions to ancient Greek civilization. The great poet Homer was Ionian.

Isolation is the state of being separated from others. For example, until they began to travel, ancient peoples lived in isolation from other groups.

J - K - L

King Agamemnon was a legendary king of Mycenae and the leader of the Greeks in the Trojan War. The Trojan War was a ten year war between the Greeks and the Trojans (the people from the city of Troy in Asia Minor). The war began when the Trojans kidnapped a woman named Helen from Greece. Helen became known as Helen of Troy.

A **lathe** is a machine used for turning and polishing wood or metals. For example, an artisan in ancient Greece used a lathe to make a table leg.

To be **liberated** means to be freed. For example, women today are more liberated than women in ancient Greece.

The **Lyceum** was an outdoor park and gymnasium where Aristotle taught. Today a lyceum is a place where lectures are given.

M

The **mainland** consists of areas of land that are not islands. For example, the mainland of Greece is the peninsula that extends into the Mediterranean Sea.

A **marathon** was a foot race run over the distance of 26 miles, 385 yards (or 42.2 kilometres).

Maritime means near the sea. For example, Greece is a maritime nation.

A **Mediterranean climate** is a climate of hot, dry summers and mild winters. For example, Greece has a Mediterranean climate.

The **middle class** refers to the people in the middle between the rich and the poor in a society. For example, ancient Greek artisans were considered middle class because they were between the aristocracy and the slaves.

The **Minoans** lived in Crete about 3000 BC. For example, the Minoans learned how to make tools from bronze.

Minted means that money has been produced by stamping it out of metal. For example, each city-state in ancient Greece minted its own coins.

Moderate means not extreme, or mild. For example, Greece has a moderate, Mediterranean climate.

Mutual consent is when people agree together. For example, in the democracies of ancient Greece, the leaders were chosen by mutual consent.

N

Nationalism means the strong feeling of belonging to a particular group or country. For example, the wars fought by ancient Greeks against a common enemy, such as the Persian Empire, encouraged a strong sense of nationalism.

Natural disaster is the term used when the forces of nature cause major destruction of people or property. Natural disasters include earthquakes, mudslides, tidal waves, volcanic eruptions, tornadoes, and hurricanes.

O

An **oligarchy** is a government controlled by a few wealthy people. For example, some ancient philosophers believed that an oligarchy was a better system of rule than a democracy.

An **oracle** was a person who could speak with a god to learn about the future. Oracle can also refer to a shrine (a place of worship). For example, the oracle at Delphi refers to the shrine of Apollo as well as the priestess there who consulted the gods.

An **orator** is a person who is good at giving formal, public speeches. For example, in ancient Athens, a person on trial could ask an orator to present the case to the jurymen.

An **orchestra** was the area in front of the seats in a theatre where the chorus danced and chanted. Today, orchestra refers to the people who make music with their voices or with musical instruments, and the orchestra pit is where they are located.

Ostracism means banishment or removal from a group. For example, ostracism was a form of punishment in ancient Greece.

P

A **paedogogos** was a family slave who was the guardian to the children and took them to school. Today, the word pedagogue, meaning teacher, comes from the Greek word paedogogos.

Pankration was a violent, no-holds barred combination of wrestling and boxing. For example, a favourite activity for some boys in ancient Greece was pankration.

Papyrus was an ancient writing material from Egypt made from the fibres of plants. For example, in ancient Greece, some school children wrote on papyrus.

A **patron** is a protector who supports a person or group of people. For example, ancient Greece had many patron gods. The people believed that these gods watched over and protected them.

A **peninsula** is a portion of land surrounded by water on three sides and connected to the mainland on the fourth. For example, Greece is a peninsula.

The **pentathlon** is an athletic contest made up of five events. The winner is the person with the highest total score for all events. For example, in ancient Greece, the pentathlon consisted of the long jump, the discus, the javelin, wrestling, and the 185 metre dash.

The **perioeci** was one of the three classes of people in Sparta. Perioeci were free but they had no vote. For example, the perioeci included artisans and farmers.

A **petasos** was a wide-brimmed felt hat. For example, in ancient Greece, a traveller might wear a petasos.

A **phalanx** is a battle formation. For example, ancient Greek hoplites formed a phalanx when they marched side by side with their shields joined and their spears overlapping each other.

Philosophers study philosophy. Philosophy uses reason and argument to find truth and knowledge. It is based on human reasoning and the love of wisdom. For example, Socrates was one of the world's greatest philosophers.

The **Phoenicians** lived in Asia at the eastern end of the Mediterranean Sea where Syria and Lebanon are now. The Greek alphabet was borrowed from the Phoenicians.

Pictography is a form of writing in which symbols and pictures represent letters, ideas, or words. For example, archaeologists have found pictographic writing on many of the vases made by the ancient Greeks.

A **plectrum** is a small piece of ivory, horn, or metal used to pluck a lyre, guitar, or mandolin. For example, Sappho invented the plectrum to pluck the strings of a lyre.

A **port** is a place where ships can dock. For example, the ancient Greeks built ports on the mainland to help them ship goods throughout the Mediterranean world.

A **portico** is a kind of porch with columns before the entrance of a building. For example, before entering a temple, the ancient Greeks had to pass through the portico.

Principles are basic beliefs. For example, laws in a democracy are based on the principles of freedom and equality.

To **prosper** is to thrive. For example, without the use of slaves, ancient Greek society could not have prospered.

A **psychologist** studies how people think. For example, psychologists study the human mind and behaviour.

Punches are tools that make holes. For example, ancient Greek sculptors used punches to create designs in marble.

Q - R

Rites are the formal ceremonies of a religion. For example, on festival days, the ancient Greeks performed special religious rites.

S

Sacred means religious, or holy. For example, to the ancient Greeks, the inside of their temples were sacred places.

A **sanctuary** is a place of protection. For example, during times of fighting, ancient Greeks moved to the acropolis to take sanctuary.

A **satyr** play is a kind of ancient Greek comedy. It is called a satyr play because it has a chorus of singers dressed up as satyrs (which are woodland deities that were half human and half horse). The satyr helped develop a modern kind of play called a farce. A farce is a play full of absurd events and situations.

Scarce means not plentiful. For example, fertile land was scarce in ancient Greece.

A **scholar** is a person who is well educated. For example, some sons of wealthy parents in ancient Athens studied with the most important scholars in their society.

Serfs are slaves who work the land for their owners. Serfs were passed on with the land from owner to owner.

A **sexist** society is one in which freedoms and duties are assigned because of a person's sex. For example, in ancient Greek society, some men could vote but women could not.

A **siege** is a military plan where the attackers surround a fortified place and try to starve the people out. For example, ancient Greeks retreated to the acropolis when their city-state was under siege.

Similarities are characteristics that people or things have in common.

Sirens are sea goddesses in mythology. Sirens sang and lured sailors to their deaths.

Smelted means that raw ore was melted so it could be made into metals. For example, one job in ancient Greece was smelting metals.

Smiths are people who work with metal. For example, iron smiths in ancient Greece made iron into tools and weapons.

A **sociologist** studies how groups of people live and act.

A **specialist** does one thing very well. For example, in ancient Greece historians wrote about Greek life, but they were specialists in the history of war.

A **staple** item is basic, or most important. For example, olives were one of the staple foods of ancient Greece.

Status refers to position or rank within a group. For example, statesmen had the highest status in ancient Greece.

A **strigil** was a flat scraping tool used by the ancient Greeks to remove olive oil and dirt from their bodies.

A **surplus** is what is left over after everyone's needs are met. For example, like other civilizations, the ancient Greeks wanted to trade their surplus food for goods that they needed.

A **symposium** was an after-dinner party for men in ancient Greece. For example, the men of Athens often met at a symposium and discussed what was happening in the political life of their city-state.

T

Technologies are ways of doing something, the methods of using science in industry or daily living. For example, the civilization of ancient Greece prospered partly because the people were able to discover and use new technologies.

Terraced means layered. For example, ancient Greek farmers planted the sides of hills in terraced rows to make the most use of limited fertile land and mountainous terrain.

A **tragedy** is a drama dealing with human unhappiness. For example, ancient Greeks gathered in the theatre to watch tragedies in which the actors faced terrible problems.

Trinkets are small fancy items or bits of jewellery. For example, ancient Greeks honoured the deities by placing trinkets in their temples.

Triremes were powerful military ships used by the ancient Greeks. On the bow of the triremes was a bronze-tipped battering ram, which could easily slice through a wooden ship.

The **Trojan Horse** was a wooden horse given as a gift to the Trojans by the Greeks in the Trojan War. Greek soldiers hid inside the horse. When the Trojans pulled the horse into the walls of their city, the Greek soldiers came out and destroyed Troy.

A **truce** is an agreement to stop fighting. For example, a truce was called during the ancient Olympic games so that all fighting between city-states stopped and people could travel to the site of the games.

To **turn** is to rotate or spin. For example, the ancient Greeks turned a piece of wood on a lathe to make a table leg.

A **tyrant** is a ruler. Today the term tyrant brings to mind a cruel ruler. But in ancient Greece, it was the name for a person who had absolute power.

U-V

A **university** is an educational institution. Today, universities give degrees in subjects such as literature, history, and science.

Utensils are instruments or tools. For example, the ancient Greeks ate with utensils that are different from the ones we use today.

W-X-Y-Z

Weaving is a process for making cloth from thread. Women did the weaving in ancient Greece.

Western means from Europe or America. For example, Western civilization refers to the culture and social and political organization of countries in Europe or America.

Index

Credits

Editorial: Nancy Foulds, Leah-Ann Lymer, Melanie Johnson, Jennifer Keane

Typesetting & Design: Pièce de Résistance Ltée., Edmonton, AB

Maps: Wendy Johnson, Johnson Cartographics, Edmonton, AB

Illustrations: Yu Chao

Lithography: Neville Lomberg

Printing: Quality Color Press, Edmonton, AB

Index: Adrian Mather

We have made every effort to correctly identify and credit the sources of all photographs, illustrations, and information used in this textbook. Reidmore Books appreciates any further information or corrections; acknowledgment will be given in subsequent editions.

Photos: Entries are by page number, coded as follows: T = Top   B = Bottom L = Left   R = Right

page
8   Lorraine O. Schultz
17   Megapress Images, Montreal, QC
        Photo by Loucas Torosis
23   Don Eastman
49   Joyce Gregory Wyels
50   Photo Search Ltd., Edmonton, AB
        Photo by Sheila Nielsen
76   Virginia Grimes
121   T-Don Eastman
        B-James Aveson
122   David Irvine
141   Lorraine O. Schultz

Back Cover: Fishermen discuss the day's catch at a market in Mykonos. Photo Search Ltd., Edmonton, AB Photo by Sheila Nielsen